THE
ULTIMATE
PRAYER ROOM
WARRIOR

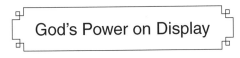

God's Power on Display

Pastor Simeon Dixon

THE ULTIMATE PRAYER ROOM WARRIOR
GOD'S POWER ON DISPLAY

iUniverse books may be ordered through booksellers or by contacting:

iUniverse
1663 Liberty Drive
Bloomington, IN 47403
www.iuniverse.com
844-349-9409

Because of the dynamic nature of the internet, any web addresses or links contained in this book may have changed since publication and may no longer be valid. The views expressed in this work are solely those of the author and do not necessarily reflect the views of the publisher, and the publisher hereby disclaims any responsibility for them.

Any people depicted in stock imagery provided by Getty Images are models, and such images are being used for illustrative purposes only.
Certain stock imagery © Getty Images.

Scripture quotations marked KJV are from the Holy Bible, King James Version (Authorized Version). First published in 1611. Quoted from the KJV Classic Reference Bible, Copyright © 1983 by The Zondervan Corporation

ISBN: 978-1-6632-2757-7 (sc)
ISBN: 978-1-6632-2759-1 (hc)
ISBN: 978-1-6632-2758-4 (e)

Library of Congress Control Number: 2021920342

Print information available on the last page.

iUniverse rev. date: 09/27/2021

CONTENTS

ONE
THE CHURCH MOTHER

THERE ARE SIMILARITIES between mothers and the church (which is the body of Christ), as well as the intercessor. These fundamental similarities have their roots in the divine. Because they are divinely orchestrated, only the divine can reveal the ultimate connection and the interacting functioning of these entities. Jesus said, "How be it when He, the Spirit of truth is come, He will guide you into all truth: for He shall not speak of Himself; but whatsoever He hears that shall He speak: and He will show you things to come" (John 16:13)[1].

By intercession, truth is revealed, the enemy's plot is destroyed, and the people of God are brought to safety and victory. King Hezekiah hesitated to present the letter of threat he received from King Sennacherib of Assyria before the Lord on the altar in the temple of the God of heaven.

> And Hezekiah prayed before the lord, and said, O Lord
> God of Israel, which dwells between the cherubims, thou

---

[1] All scriptural references are from the King James Version of the Bible.

1

art the God, even thou alone, of all the kingdoms of the earth; Thou hast made the heaven and earth.

Lord, bow down thine ear, and hear: open, LORD, thine eyes, and see: and hear the words of Sennachherb, which hath sent him, to reproach the living God. Of a truth, Lord, the kings of Assyria have destroyed the nations and their lands, and have cast their gods into the fire: for they were no gods, but the work of man's hands, wood and stone. Therefore they have destroyed them. Now therefore, O Lord our God, I beseech thee, save thou us out of his hand, that all the kingdoms of the earth may know that thou art the Lord God, even thou only. (2 Kings 19:15–19)

The king was conceived with a desire to see God and His people vindicated. Therefore, he travailed in a prayer and intercession, and God responded to his cry and delivered them. The prophet Elijah, by intercession, returned the heart of the backsliding nation of Israel to God after he gathered them together with King Ahab and his false prophets upon Mount Carmel (1 Kings 18).

When a believer intercedes in true sincerity, God will always respond with a positive answer.

The intercessor is the reproductive organ of the church. The church is the mother. "But Jerusalem which is above is free, which is the mother of us all" (Galatians 4:26). The church travails in prayer to give birth to lost sinners. Likewise, the intercessors travail in order that the body of Christ remains safe, healthy, and strong.

I was in a season of intercession when the Spirit of the Lord made it known to me that the intercessor is the womb of the church. It has been said that a woman is a man with a womb. The purpose of the womb is to bring forth new life into the world.

The prophet Isaiah wrote, "Who hath heard such a thing? Who hath seen such things? Shall the earth be made to bring forth in one day? Or shall a nation be born at once? For as soon as Zion travailed, she brought forth her children" (Isaiah 66:8).

The church brings forth from time to time because she travails in birth pains through intercession. Motherhood is one of the most challenging experiences from its very inception in the garden of Eden. Not only does the mother give birth to the children, but she nurtures and protects, and she sustains her young. She has an unbreakable tie to every child that she bears.

The word *mother* takes us back to the dawn of creation. This tells us that the word *mother* represents the life-producing, life-sustaining, and life-preserving entity. Without the mother, the reproductive source of life would be nonexistent. Mother, therefore, is a priceless species, which is above all others in the human realm. She carries within herself some of God's most undiscovered goodnesses.

These qualities are highly necessary for the further development of humankind. History shows that men in leadership have failed time and time again to give recognition to some of the important roles that mothers have played in the church. Not only were they denied but they were also blatantly ignored or falsely accused.

Our enemy, Satan, has successfully and devastatingly blinded some of our prominent men down throughout history. They have failed to recognize God's intended plan of partnership with His women in the church. There is a mystery between God and His women, which He has eventually gotten through to some of His male servants in the body of Christ.

This mystery becomes open only to the men who have spent much yielding of their time to God in prayer, fasting, and careful study of His word. Any man who can elevate the spirit of his wife into the presence of God and keep her there has found himself a complete woman. All that she has, all that she is, and all that she will ever be will be totally surrendered to him.

"Even as Sarah obeyed Abraham, calling him Lord" (1 Peter 3:6a). Men are little gods, and we are great at creating monsters out of our women. The nature of the woman is to engage in the things that give her a sense of elevation. She is closest to being her total self when and only when she is in the presence of God.

The power of her creativity comes alive when she is being recognized and honored for who she is. When there is total understanding and acceptance of both species, the reproductive spirit and power of God will meet and connect with the earthly creatures. In this meeting, yielded earthly, fleshy creatures become like God in the earth (His nature and character). We act like God, we speak like God, and we will conquer the enemy's territories like God said we should.

This is the power that drives the intercessors into the very presence of God. The vision of the individual becomes clearer in times of intercession. Our ability to produce is no longer obscured when we intercede. When we encounter bareness, drought, or lack of growth in the church, the Spirit of God rises up violently in us and launches victorious attacks on the kingdom of darkness.

It is in this state of darkness that Satan plans his attack upon the church. If he is left alone, he will abort every baby who is being conceived in the church—first, the physical and then the spiritual. The heathens practiced these kinds of behaviors centuries before Christ came. Jeremiah spoke out against it in Jeremiah 19:4–5.

> Because they have forsaken me, and have estranged this place, and have burned incense in it, unto other gods, whom neither they nor their fathers have known, nor the kings of Judah, and have filled this place with the blood of innocents; they have built also the high places of Baal, to burn their sons with fire for burnt offerings

unto Baal, which I commanded not, nor spoke it, neither came it into my mind.

Where Israel had forsaken God, the believers forsake the altar of prayer and intercession. The incense, which a backsliding Israel burned, is the representation of the intercessions of the believers of today. Where the blood of the innocents flowed, the blood of the souls of the spiritually unborn is flowing in the church today. This accounts for the lack of church growth and for the barrenness and spiritual death.

The intercessor must hover over the prophetic word of God. These are the promises that God has given to us through the preached word. The intercession brings the increase into the family of God.

The prophet Joel forewarned, "Let the priest, the ministers of the Lord, weep between the porch and the altar, and let them say, spare thy people, O Lord, and give not thine heritage to reproach, that the heathen should reign over them" (Joel 2:17).

It is very reproachful when a married woman fails to produce a child. This is her ardent hope; this is the deepest desire of her husband. The parents of both the bride and groom look with great anticipation, waiting and planning for a time of celebration, only to be disappointed by the failure to produce.

The ministry of intercession has been largely explored and sustained by the female population of the church, from of old. Few men have tapped into this reservoir. Men have limited themselves in this regard and sometimes played havoc against women who have or would have dedicated themselves to this unique ministry.

We seem to have forgotten the instruction "That by supplications, prayers, intercessions, and giving of thanks … we would lead a peaceable life with all godliness and honesty. God accepting this, He would have all men to be saved" (1 Timothy 2:1–4). In verse 8, he said, "I will therefore that men ought to pray everywhere, lifting up holy hands, without wrath and doubting."

I have noticed in recorded history and in our times that some men have become hindrances to the women in their lives or the ministry of intercession. The women were criticized and even accused of seeking self-exaltation. This has become an age-old problem, which can be traced back to the time of the patriarchs, the priests, and the prophets.

In the story of Hannah, we learned that she was barren. She was an unproductive woman. Though this was an accident at birth, it was also a curse. Curses bring sorrow. Curses bring displacements. Curses bring death.

The mystery between God and His women begins to be revealed in this story. Traditionally, it was out of character for anyone, besides the priest, to offer petitions to God, let alone a woman. But Hannah found out that she could do something about her barrenness, so she did.

It has been said that every Christian was called to reproduce him- or herself. Those of us who have done something about it have become producers in the body of Christ. Hannah never allowed her barrenness to dictate her lifestyle, nor alter her destiny. Neither did she accept the traditions of men.

Tradition is a chain that binds us. It is a scale that blinds our eyes. And it is a weapon, which if we do not seek to escape from it, will kill us. Hannah was stigmatized, ridiculed, and scandalized in a world that was paralyzed by traditions.

As we look closely, we find that her childlessness did not altogether affect her productivity. She discovered that not only was she a physical human being who had a connection to the earthly human race but that there was a more important part of her that was being connected to the divine and the supernatural.

She had to have made this discovery on her own, because her husband, Elkannah, tried to stop her and to get her to settle for the obvious. Flesh and blood did not reveal this to her.

We also see in the story that male covering, which God had provided her with, had failed her miserably. What then could a woman do but search within herself for an answer to the impossibility she was faced with?

Hannah, being the woman and the prospective mother she was, went into the secret place of the Most High, and she made an eye-opening discovery, a discovery that lasted from generation to generation.

She prayed:

> And she vowed a vow and said, O Lord of host, if thou wilt indeed look on the affliction of thine handmaid, and remember me, and not forget thine handmaid, but will give unto thine handmaid a man child, then I will give him unto the lord all the days of his life, and there shall no razor come upon his head. (Samuel 1:11)

Hannah discovered her spirituality. She also discovered the purpose of her true existence. She went into the presence of the Most High with an attitude of worship. True worship demands a sacrifice.

A true worshipper is an unselfish person. Hannah was totally unselfish in her request. She was completely sold out to God. That which she sought after was not to be her own anymore; it was supposed to be God's.

This kind of request will always get God's attention. Hannah's unselfish gift to God became Israel's defense against their enemies and their intercessor before God. The spirit of intercession, which resided in Hannah, was passed on to her son, Samuel.

Hannah's birth pains began before the conception of her son. In her travailing, Eli, the priest, observed her closely. He saw her lips moving as if she were muttering like an inebriated individual.

His conclusion of the matter was totally unfounded. His accusation of her being a drunkard only added to the piles of rejection that she encountered continually.

> And Eli said to her, "How long wilt thou be drunken? Put away thy wine from thee." With the pains in her eyes and the trembling in her voice, she muttered to Eli the priest, no, my Lord, I am a woman of a sorrowful spirit.
>
> I have drunken neither wine nor strong drink, but have poured out my soul before the Lord. Count not thine handmaid for a daughter of Belial: for out of the abundance of my complaint and grief have I spoken hitherto. (1 Samuel 1:14)

Hannah taught us a very valuable lesson that brought enlightenment to the sacrificial gift, which always gets God's attention. Her praying must have caused her to become a carrier of God's presence.

What an impact she must have had upon her son! She had gracefully opened up to him the true source of power for living. She made a connection for young Samuel. I wish that every mother and father would do whatever it takes for his or her children.

Hannah beat all odds. She did not defy spiritual authority. She was submissive but resolute in her faith in God. She must have said, "The God who made me with a nonproductive womb can alter the intricacies and change it to be conducive to my desires in His will."

She unknowingly coined the phrase "Whatsoever you desire when you pray, believe that you receive it and you shall have it." Hannah could have resigned herself to her unfortunate condition, like so many of us today do.

We say, "I was not called to be an intercessor, so why bother?" or "I was not called to be a soul winner, why bother? I was not called to go on the mission field overseas, so I have resolved I will just attend church services, and that is enough."

What we are doing in these cases is accepting our barrenness. Hannah sought after and obtained the fertilizing power of the Holy Spirit of God, and so can we. We were born into the kingdom of God to reproduce ourselves.

We have miserably fallen into the bed of complacency. We have become like Jonah. We have gone down into the bottom of the ship and have fallen asleep. Or like Saul, we are hiding behind things.

"And that, knowing the time, that now it is high time to awake out of sleep: for now is our salvation nearer than when we believed" (Romans 13:11).

Every born-again child of God has that reproductive ability. We only need to apply ourselves to the Spirit of God, and He will fertilize us. He will take away our barrenness, and He will fertilize us. He will make us to be reproductive—even as Hannah, Sarah, and Elizabeth. If we do not populate as we ought to, then the wild beasts will outpopulate and destroy us.

TWO
A TRAUMATIC CHILDHOOD

MY PARENTS TOGETHER had sixteen children. I am the eighth child and the first boy. It is a father's delight that his first child should be a boy. For my father, it was not to be. Mother said she was always hoping to have a son when she first became pregnant. It was not so.

My mother's name was Melvina, but she was affectionately called "Mel."

Mother tells of her quest to have a boy child; she said that after so many pregnancies and seven girls (which were born to my parents) that she was never going to give birth to a son. Nevertheless, she continued to pray and fast.

Again, she got pregnant. In those days, a mother had to wait for nine long months before she knew the gender of her baby. She said that was the longest nine months of all her pregnancies. This pregnancy was quite different. It was different because she had two expectancies: one from conception of the baby and the other from the conception of faith.

She knew she had touched God through prayers and fasting, which she offered daily. She tells of the newness of her convictions and the assurance of her faith that God did hear her and would answer her prayers.

She counted the days to the delivery. The midwife was a highly spiritual woman. She was a woman who devoted herself in prayer and fasting continually. She prophesied to my mother that she was going to have a son, and she was right.

From a place of peace and comfort, safety and tranquility, I was placed in a very hostile environment. It seemed like there was neither welcome nor place for me in this world. It was plain to see that if I was going to live on this planet, learning the skills of daily warfare was unavoidable. The forces of hell had organized against me, but my mother kept me covered in prayer while my father taught me the word.

I was loved by my parents and siblings. Although it was not spoken frequently, I knew they loved me by the expressions they directed toward me. When I was a youth, I had many health challenges. In the months of June and July, the pollen from the corn blossoms would cause me to break out in a skin rash.

These rashes would sometimes develop into petrifying sores. Some of my schoolmates and colleagues scorned and laughed at me. They treated me with disdain. I cried and lamented because I was hurting. I felt rejected whenever I went outside my home circle. I became unsociable.

Being the good parents that they were, my father and my mother loved me passionately. They were extremely attentive to me. They gave me all the attention I needed throughout every enduring episode of my terrifying experiences.

I had some agonizing trauma on many nights, and every time that they heard my voice, my parents would be by my bedside.

I grew up to understand that the love of God was being expressed in my young life. My parents were divinely chosen for me. I believe that

God had specially selected them to have and raise me. Their diligence in watching, praying, and hovering over me was of genuine totality.

My sisters all pampered me. They were at my beckoning as often as possible. I believe that they too were compelled and driven by God's unconditional love. Their compassion and devotion were second to none.

When I could not sleep at night, they were awoken either by my crying or by my mother's prayers. My three brothers, who followed me in sequence, cared deeply for me also. They also experienced similar situations, as you will read later on in this book.

My father was very proud of me. He took me with him almost everywhere he went. One day, he took me and one of my sisters with him to the field. While he was working, my sister watched to make sure that I was safe from dangers. It was lunchtime, and my father called us to the eating place.

We all sat down to eat. Most of the food and vegetables we ate were grown on my father's farm. He was a very good farmer. That day, after lunch, Papa went back to work, while my sister and I went back to playing. It was now afternoon, slowly approaching time for us to go home.

It began raining, so we had to shelter in a nearby hut. Papa made us umbrellas from the thatch leaves so we could shelter from the drenching rain while running toward the hut. By the time he got through making the umbrellas, we were soaked.

We were approximately two and a half miles from home. After the rains ceased, we were invaded by mosquitoes, which came down in swarms. I was stung all over my body.

Shortly thereafter, I began to be uncomfortable. I was itching in every exposed area of my body and even where I was covered by my clothes. My constant crying caught the attention of my father, who responded, "What's wrong with you, Man?"

"The mosquitoes are biting me, sir," I sobbed.

"Do you want to go home?" he asked.

"Yes, sir."

His questioning me filled my mind with great anticipation. At that juncture, all that I wanted was to go home to the warm embrace of my mother.

He stopped working and walked briskly toward me. He was rather surprised to see how swollen I had become. He sent me and my sister home. While we were on our way home, the rains came in torrential downpours again.

On reaching home, I was roasting with fever. Mother was shocked and angry. She thought that at the age of six years old, keeping me in the field for a whole day was too much. Also, it was a known fact that I had health problems, which were connected to pollen from the trees and plants.

Mama gave me some homemade remedies, which she hoped would bring down my temperature. By the following morning, the fever had left me, but the swelling was still severe. Both of my eyes were swollen shut.

I could not see even the sunlight. My sister, the one I followed in the sibling sequence, led me to the breakfast table and then back to my bed. I cannot recall if my mother prayed then, but as I was growing up later, I knew she prayed about everything.

The swelling disappeared in a couple of days, and I was back to my normal life, jolly and playful.

My parents spoke to me about my future: I wanted to do tailoring, to design and sew men's suits. I told my brother he should be the carpenter. I would design his suits, and he would build my house. We had our plans and wanted to bring them to fruition.

The devil is a stealer and destroyer of dreams. Mine were no exception, especially the way he targeted me from birth. I was on top of his hit list, it seemed.

I enrolled in school, and my first year began. I was jumped by a bully the first day that I attended. He worked me over quite badly. The second day, he attacked me again. This time, I took care of the matter rather efficiently or ineffectively.

I hurt him badly, and in the process, I set a record that stayed with me for the rest of my school years. No one who knew or heard of that incident dared try to attack me or any one of my family members again.

That boy set out to bully me, and I recognized it and put a stop to it right away; so also did the devil seek to bully me as well, but walking in my mother's footsteps as an intercessor, I took care of him on my knees.

I had some unforgettable experiences in my school years. Some imposed dangers of various degrees plagued me, while some of them I walked away from and was able to be victorious over.

This was due to my trust in God and faith in His word. Truth is, I was afraid of God. My parents instilled in me that God was not only angry when I misbehaved but that He was also pleased with me when I did the right thing.

At age nine, I had an unmistakable encounter with death. The viselike grip of shingles had me bound. It pulled me into its deadening grasp, and it seemed like it happened suddenly. Mother discovered those pimples, which she described as "water bumps," appearing around my waist. She was not sure what they were then or what the root cause was. After she made inquiries, by consulting the senior citizens of the area, a few people visited me. At this early stage, I was still jolly and playful. Someone told my mother that the lesions were called "shingles."

As children, we equate such a description with the house rooftops. This was somewhat puzzling to my young mind. Having been told of the severity of the lesions, Mother took me to see the family doctor who served our community. In those days, doctors were assigned to a community once per week at the health clinic as the general practitioner.

It was Wednesday afternoon, nearing to the time when children would be discharged from school. We had to pass the school to get to the doctor's office.

It was embarrassing for me because my classmates and the other children who knew me laughed at me, as I was absent from school. Knowing the stigma they attached to me from the skin rash heightened my fear and timidity. But in my mother's presence, they dared not interfere with me.

We passed the school and arrived at the clinic. The veranda was packed with patients who were waiting to see the doctor. Everyone was waiting his or her turn.

When it was my turn to be checked by my doctor, Mother pulled me up to her and tucked in my shirt. She said, "Come on, Son. It's your turn."

We both walked into the doctor's office.

I can remember the big brown door closing behind us with a loud clunk. We walked down the short hallway to another door, where he beckoned us in. He picked me up and placed me on his examining table.

"Hi, Man, how are you doing today?" the doctor asked.

I bowed my head in shyness and held my peace. I did not want to say anything because I was afraid that he was going to give me an injection. I was rather terrified by the shiny needle. Mama took that question and stretched it into a long conversation, which was mixed with more intense questions and opinions.

These questions were her own conclusions. The doctor, with his right hand across his chest supporting his left elbow, and the palm of his left hand massaging his cheeks, listened quite attentively to Mother for a period of time, and then he interjected.

He educated Mother on his professional discovery and gave a blanketed answer. "The boy has a rare disease, Mrs. Dixon, and we have no known cure for it."

"What is the name of this disease?" Mama asked.

"It is known as *shingles*. The little that we know about this lesion is that if it meets together around his waist, he will not recover."

I could see my mother's countenance change. I did not know what "recover" meant, but in my childhood thinking, I thought that meant I would die.

After the conversation concluded, the doctor gave her some medicine, and we took off for home. My father was not yet home from the field when we got in. Mother sat down and then called one of my sisters to fetch her some drinking water.

Papa got home to find my mother in a posture he was not accustomed to. She was sitting on a big rock in the yard. Her left hand was resting on her breasts while her right elbow was seated in the palm of her left hand. She supported her chin with her middle, ring, and little fingers while her index finger and her thumb supported her cheeks.

With much eagerness, Papa unloaded the load he had on his head and then briskly stepped over to her. He rested his right hand on her left shoulder and asked compassionately, "Mel, what is wrong?"

With tears running down her beautiful cheeks, she muttered to Dad, "Doctor said he cannot help him."

It was then that my siblings found out that there was a good chance they could lose their eldest brother.

Papa was in disbelief. After a brief conversation, he lit his pipe and walked down to the coffee and banana farm. I did not think he wanted us to see him crying, and so he excused himself. One of my brothers attempted to follow him, but he told him not to come with him this time.

With the evening chores being ended, it was bedtime. We all knew that we had to pray before we went off to bed. Papa reached for his big black Bible, opened it up, and began to read. After reading, he fetched the *Sacred Songs* songbook, and we all began to sing.

After we sang so many songs, Papa exhorted us from the scriptures, and Mother led us, one by one, to pray in our own words. After we were through, Papa prayed. He cried his eyes out. Then Mama took over. She went into one of those long, lamenting prayers she always prayed.

When my mother prayed, you didn't know if it was winter or summer because chill bumps came up all over your body—at least they did on mine. Her prayers became intense and consistent.

The lesion continued to grow until it got to a distance of approximately one and a half inches of meeting. My father monitored the condition of the lesion daily.

One morning, after he checked me over, he exclaimed to Mother, "Mel, the shingles did not grow any further last night!" It seems the pimples grew more rapidly at night than during the day.

She reached out for me, pulled me closer, and said, "Thank you, Jesus! Thank you, Jesus."

Everyone gathered around to share in the excitement. She knew that God had performed a healing miracle on me again. Mother knew that there was no other possibility for me to be healed but by Jesus Christ Himself.

The doctor had given her absolutely no hope for my recovery. The danger I was facing became frightening news to the whole family. When my parents were told of the recent death of the Baptist minister, which they claimed was caused by the same condition that I had, they became bewildered. He had shingles around his neck, which connected, and he died.

I then noticed that I had neighbors and family visiting me from the district, which had never happened so frequently. They often gathered in groups and sang, read scriptures, and prayed. I got all the attention that I could ever want.

I was not aware that those visits were meant to show their last respects and expressions of love. My eldest sister, who was away from home, came visiting also. Though I was given lots of goodies, they wept bitterly before returning to their jobs in the city.

Now I can say after so many years, maturely, "Glory to God." The lesions began to dry up. The severe pains were alleviated. What I had experienced then was that the lesion came with three major sensations: sometimes pain with a crippling grasp, a burning sensation that sent shock waves throughout the body, and then an itching, which spread like electrical wildfire running through my veins.

After two or three attempts of scratching, it multiplies and then engulfs the whole body in an uncontrollable misery. This throws the body into an unrelenting and unexplainable sensation. It is like tongues of a flame leaping from a burning sugarcane field. It is like hell in the human body.

Mother took me back to see the family doctor. He was surprised to see that I was still alive. He said to her, "What did you give him? Because I know that medicine would not get him better." They talked for a while, and then he gave her some ointment for the itching. That did work, and I got totally well again. To God be the glory.

THREE
IT IS POSSIBLE TO KNOW GOD

WE READ IN Daniel 11:34, "The people that do know their God shall be strong and do exploits." Mother knew God in a very special way. She spent quality time with Him. She was constantly in prayer, worship, thanksgiving, and praising God.

Mother was a true worshipper of the Lord. Not long after my healing from the shingles, one of my brothers, Joseph, became ill. He was stricken with a severe fever and cold. Mother gave him some of her homemade remedy as was her custom. That was not effective, so she took him to the doctor.

The doctor told her that she had waited too long to take the child to him. He displayed a mild anger toward Mother because of the deterioration of her child's health.

"Why didn't you take the child to the hospital emergency room?"

With tears in her eyes, she responded, "Doctor, I did not have the money to hire a car to get him there."

"Because of the delay," the doctor said, "there is a slim chance of this child surviving this fever. Mrs. Dixon, your son has a bad case of pneumonia."

Mother broke down and began to cry. He gave her some medicine and sent us home. The doctor cautioned her to be careful to keep the rest of us children away from Joseph, because we could be contaminated. "You may bring him back next week if he is still alive," the doctor said.

Mother and I walked out of the doctor's office with her dying son, my brother, wrapped up in a blanket. We had to walk approximately two and a half miles to get home. Mother prayed that the rain would not come. It would have been sudden death for Joseph if he should get wet by the rains.

She trudged her way home. When she got into the house, she laid him in the bed and went about doing her wifely and motherly chores. When Father got home from the field, my mother gave him the report.

His countenance fell, and then he burst into tears. He said, "Well, well, you did pray for Manager [that's me], and God healed him, so we will pray again. Maybe He will heal Levy also." Joseph's pet name was Levy.

That evening, Mother called the family together, and we sang hymns, songs, and choruses. She led us into the worship. My father read from the Holy Bible. Afterward, he explained to us the best way he could. Mother led us to pray one by one from the youngest to the eldest child.

After we children got through praying, it was Father's turn. He wept bitterly before God, on his knees, as he cried out to Him for mercy for my brother. Listening closely while each of us prayed, I remembered how differently Mama's prayers were from those of even my father.

In so many ways, her prayers were uniquely expressed. She first recognized God's love and mercy toward us and also His might and the power by which He worked in the universe.

She would lead off with a high level of worship and then go into a series of praises with her arms raised above her head, swaying from side to side. She shouted loud praises, "Hallelujahs," and glories to God.

This caused strange feelings to penetrate my body. My heart would palpitate much faster as if to burst my chest. Sometimes those feelings got so strong, I burst out crying. Knowing not what to make of those feelings then, I pondered them in my heart.

I wanted to pray just like my mother did because of the intensity of her prayers. They were always lengthy. After she got through worshiping, praising, and thanking God for everything or anything, then she began praying. Mother made requests before the Lord for everyone she could remember and for those she did not know.

She would often quote verses from the Bible and from songs that she memorized from just listening to my Father reading to her. Her requests before God were like those of the preachers of old.

Days went by, and Joseph was still alive. We held a constant vigil at his bedside. Mother tried to keep us away from him, but it was virtually impossible to do so. His hallucinations sometimes caused us to laugh hilariously and also to cry bitterly. We did not want to lose our brother.

There was nothing we could do. We felt helpless, angry, and frustrated. The same week of Joseph's visit to the doctor, my youngest brother, Emmanuel, became ill with the same illness that threatened Joseph's life.

"When it rains, it pours." Now, Mother had two sick children to care for at the same time. My mother was a strong woman though petite in size. With a limited amount of money, my parents had to decide which of the sick children they should take to the doctor.

The week whisked by, and it was Wednesday again, so Mother decided to take Emmanuel to see the doctor. The routines were the same. We sat and waited for our turn to see the practitioner. We were early this time.

We sat on one of the rows of long benches. Up drove the doctor. He reached for his bag in the back seat of his car and headed toward the office. Everything was well arranged by the nurse. Names were called according to the patients listed from the week before.

Joseph Dixon's name was announced, and Mom got up and escorted Emmanuel in to see the doctor. He remembered us from the week before and, surprised, exclaimed, "Is he still alive?"

"Yes, Doctor," Mother replied. "But this is Emmanuel, not Joseph."

"What happened to Joseph? Is he still alive?" the doctor inquired.

Mother responded with a broad smile on her face. "Yes, Doctor."

The doctor replied, "Then if Joseph is still alive, take Emmanuel home, and whatever you did for Joseph, do the same for this one."

He gave us medicine and then sent us home. We went back home, and Mother did the same thing for the current situation. Prayer was her daily food. She ate, breathed, and lived prayer.

There was no transaction done in the home without a prayer covering over it. We offered up prayer again, on behalf of Emmanuel, my brother, and God came in one more time and performed a healing miracle.

My father was a very brilliant man. He told us he had memorized one thousand questions and answers from the Bible.

At the beginning of each school year, we got our new textbooks. As soon as we got through having dinner, he took us one by one each evening and read through each textbook.

After he read it through, for the rest of the year, we could ask him any questions we chose from any particular book. He would give the answer, sometimes verbatim.

He had shared with us an incident in his time at school when he was a boy. The teacher assigned a portion of scriptures for the class to memorize for homework. He did not do his homework. When he got to school the following morning, the teacher called the class to form a line to check their reports.

He said he was the second boy from the front of the line. Before the test began, the teacher turned to her desk to get something. By the time she had turned around, he had slipped behind the student who was behind him, becoming the third student in line.

By the time the students in front of him got through struggling to repeat the verse, he had learned it then. Thus he avoided a whipping from the teacher.

As fascinated as I was by my father's brilliance, my mother's memory startled me. How could someone who could not read a word in print be so sharp? Mother had such a hunger for God and the truth contained in His word that just by listening to the scriptures being read, she captured so much.

It was almost unbelievable. Whenever she got back home from church or any religious meeting, she would ask my father, who was always willing to read the scriptures that were taken as text at the meetings to her. She also memorized whole hymns, songs, and choruses.

Mother's prayers were always fervent. Whenever she got through praying, one was left with a feeling that can be likened to the way one feels after taking a much-needed bath. She left you feeling refreshed, renewed, revived, and rejuvenated.

There seemed to be some work of transformation that took place each time she prayed. Mother had a personal relationship with God. My thoughts of her abiding in the presence of the Most Holy One were that *I wanted to know God the way she knew Him.*

This desire brought a series of questions to my young mind. Father told us that God is a Spirit and that we could never see Him with our natural, physical eyes. How then, I wondered, would I know Him when and if I found Him? *Where should I begin to look? If God is all the way up in heaven, does He come to visit me only when He wants to? When would I be able to meet with Him?* I thought He was hiding Himself away, and then He came only in secret. I thought only Father Christmas (Santa) played those tricks.

These thoughts and feelings remained with me for a long time. Nothing could divert my desire and my hunger for the God of my mother. Those feelings and thoughts from my youth have never left me. They are fresh on my mind as if it were yesterday that I processed them.

The vagueness, the uncertainties, the ignorance, never diminished my hunger, my thirst for a loving, merciful, and gracious God. If only I could find Him, if only I could see Him, if only I could come to know Him like my mother did, then I would be happy. I would be as peaceful and as contented as my mother was.

My pursuit began. It was a road I knew not, a road to be marked by perils. It was a road with curves, valleys, and steep and slippery hills. The mileage was undisclosed to me. The curves were most of the time sudden and very sharp.

There have been obstacles of all descriptions. They were enduring and threatening. Discouragements have never been absent. Turning back was never an option.

My journey began under my homemade bed, which my papa had constructed for me. This became the most secluded spot for me in the house. The bed was not so high that someone could see me at a glance. Neither was it too low for me to not be able to get under it.

Before my devotion began, I got Daddy's sacred songs and solos and my Bible, which he gave to me. I crawled under my bed. I sang, I read, and I prayed. I did this quite often until it became a routine.

I found that I started having similar feelings to the ones I used to have when my mother prayed. I did not quite understand the reality of it all. I remember that I could no longer involve myself in mischievous acts like I used to. I started having convictions about my erratic behavior, mainly in thoughts.

These new experiences only caused more unrest and confusion. I did not discuss my new experience with anyone. If I had informed my mother about my quest, she would no doubt have enlightened me. She did well in teaching us of the miraculous power of God, in performing the healings of my siblings and me.

Mother told us that God is greater than the doctors, greater than the medicines, and greater than the sickness.

"Then why did He let me and my brother get ill?"

She said, "Well, Son, God did not do any of those things. The devil did it."

I paused. Then I asked some very intriguing questions. "Who is the devil?"

Father took that question as if he knew it was coming. He explained where the devil came from, how he came to be on earth, and what his mission on the earth was about.

It was complicated for me; nevertheless, it brought some rest to my inquiring mind. I realized that it was the devil who caused me to do mischievous and unsavory things. I also learned from my papa that I must take responsibility for my actions.

I learned that Jesus Christ died on the cross for my sins. But only if I acknowledged my sin would I be forgiven. I pondered, "If the devil caused me to sin, why then should I be responsible? Why should I have to repent for those sins?"

They told me that Jesus died for me so that my sin might be forgiven. With that, I asked myself, "Why should Jesus die for me?"

Then I asked, "Papa, if God is so great and is watching over me day and night, and he loves me so much, how could this bad devil hurt me and my brothers so badly?"

Mother said, "When we obey God, He protects us from all harm and dangers, which the devil is responsible for. Sometimes after the devil hurts us, God will heal us just like He did for you and your brothers. So, you see, you do not have to be afraid."

The consolation my parents gave me was enough for me to continue my quest to find this gracious and loving God. Their instructions were scriptural, spiritually sound, and heavenly directed.

FOUR
ATTACK ON MY VISION

I WAS SITTING with a close relative at his residence. It was late in the evening. We sat and talked for a long time until it began to get dark. The animals went to lie in their resting places, the birds ceased their chirping, and the chickens flew to their roost.

While all the creatures of the day settled into their respective places, the silence of the night began to settle. There we sat on a huge rock, almost back to back. I was facing the west, and he was facing the south. Their outdoor kitchen was sitting east to west, with the front facing the east.

Looking in the westerly direction, I saw my cousin's mother walking out of the kitchen. She was coming toward us. She had a slingshot in her right hand, and her left hand was in her apron pocket. She pulled her hand out from her pocket as she walked toward us. She put a small rock in the slingshot; it was sized to fit the leather holder.

She said to her son, "Boy, you don't know how to shoot birds. Let me show you how they shoot birds."

We both became silent as we focused on her walking slowly toward us.

I wondered what she was talking about. The silence of the night was more than enough to let one know that all the birds had gone home for the night. While those thoughts were rushing through my head, she loaded the gravel into the holder of the slingshot and aimed it at me.

I sat still in wonderment. Could she be so wicked as to actually want to shoot me? I had never done any of her children any wrong. We had had no quarrels prior to this event. She pulled back on the slingshot and then let go.

That very instant, I was hit in my left eye. I screamed at the top of my little lungs. I whirled and twirled in agony. I fell off the rock and rolled on the ground. As I can remember, she offered no assistance.

I got up and tried to walk, but I could not see clearly enough, so I stood with my hand over my face. My mother needed no time to interpret whose voice it was when she heard the screams. She knew where I was. She shouted, "What's the matter, boy?"

I was in shock. I could not answer her. The next thing I knew, one of my sisters was holding me in her arms, embracing me, and she took me home. We lived about two hundred yards apart from our relatives.

Mother took me up in her arms and then lifted me onto her lap. Both my parents eagerly asked me what the matter was. I tried to tell them but with much difficulty. I wondered if it was an accident and if Mom and Dad would be angry at her or me.

Mother had warned us about going to her house because of past heartless behavior, which she had demonstrated toward other people's children.

This had to be an accident, I thought. She said she was going to show her son how to shoot birds. If she was shooting at a bird and missed, then who could blame her for a willful and cruel act?

I could not have imagined that an adult, especially a relative, could ever want to hurt me. I was an innocent child and mostly everybody's favorite. At the time of this incident, I was in third grade. I loved to read, especially the Bible.

After being shot in my eye, I could not read as often or as much as I did previously. My teachers and classmates thought of me as being a genius. It was often puzzling to them that I could come up with the meaning of words that I had never heard or read about before.

There was this voice in my head that would speak the meanings of words to me. I only knew the answer to the questions in my homework to be correct after the teachers or my father checked my schoolwork and marked them correct.

My dad used me as his notepad. He only had to tell me whatever he wanted to remember at a later date once. Whenever he was ready for the stored information, he called me, and I would recall his notes from my memory.

My reading habit and my sharp memory were vastly altered after this incident with my eye. At that tender age, I did not know the effects of my mother's intense prayers. What I can never forget was that every Sunday morning before any of us ventured out of the doors of our little home, we all gathered together in the living room for prayer.

My father tracked the hymns and songs while everyone sang together. Mother would sometimes track the songs and scriptures from memory because she could not read. Papa read aloud for everyone to hear. We listened quietly and attentively. I was losing my sight slowly.

I kept crying and complaining to my mother about my eye problem. Both my parents showed their deepest concern for me. One morning after prayers, Mother told my bigger sisters to get a five-gallon tin, wash it clean, and then fill it with clean drinking water. They set it in one of the corners of the house and covered it with a white towel.

As children, we did not know what to make of it. We watched very closely day after day and night after night. Mother announced in the

Sunday morning prayer that she was going to be fasting for nine days. We were charged to be quiet and peaceful while Mom would be on a fast.

My father was very cooperative. He came home from work earlier than usual to prepare our meals. When we got home from school, he was already home. He made sure we did not frequent the room where Mom was.

He sent us further away from the house to play. He prepared all of our meals for the entire period. He only cooked when mother was ill or at times such as that occasion. We inquired about Mom's condition, as we never fully understood what fasting was all about.

Father took delight in answering our brazen questions. Mother fasted and prayed over the container of water for nine days. She had continual prayers with the whole family nightly.

After the fasting period had ended, she used the water to wash my face every morning and at night. She opened my eyes and poured some of it in both of them. I could not tell what happened or when; all I knew was that I could see clearly again.

I went back to reading without any problems. My reading time and quality improved both at home and at school. When the eye problems got worse, Mom took me to see the doctor. He recommended a specialist who, he said, would recommend glasses. Before she took me to see the specialist, I was totally healed.

Sometimes, while we were at play, we heard Mom shouting in the house by herself. She praised the Lord with "Hallelujahs," "Glory," "Thank you, Jesus," and praises to His holy name. These periods were always loud and very repetitive.

I later came to the understanding of her unfailing gratitude to God, who never failed to answer her prayers. God has always been in attendance to my mother's desperate cries because she was a constant worshipper. She was always grateful to God for His merciful kindness and His tender mercies toward us.

FIVE
KEEPING THE FOCUS

MOTHER DID NOT have too many friends. She did not have time to gossip. She spent her time, for the most part, in the presence of God, training her children to walk in the fear of God, and keeping my father covered from harm and dangers on the job.

My father was a small farmer. He grew all of the foods that we ate except for the flour and rice. He raised his pigs and goats. I had the greater responsibility over the goats. He checked the goats once or twice per week, but I had to report to him on a daily basis. We had approximately forty heads of goats in the fields.

The pigs and the chickens were kept near the house. Of the forty head of goats, we only needed to keep five of them tied in ropes. My duty was to get up out of bed every morning at six o'clock to tend the animals before going to school.

I remember a few times when tying the goats and walking away, I saw visions of a goat dying from strangulation. There were flashes of those scenes before my face. I would then return and relocate that particular goat to a safer spot. When I told my parents of these incidences, they looked at each other and smiled.

Mom would reach out and pull me toward her. She would rub my head with the palms of her hands and say, "The Lord is with you, boy. You must be careful what you do."

I questioned, "Do you mean God is with me everywhere I go?"

Mother replied with an arousing, "Yes, everywhere you go, He is watching over you."

I did not know whether I should be glad or afraid. I was very much afraid of lightning and thunder. Whenever these occurred, it was time to curl up beside one of my parents.

If they were not close enough, I crawled under my bed and covered my head. Our parents told us that God allowed the lightning and the thunder to happen to inform us that He is in charge of everything. This made for further wondering hopelessly about this great and powerful God following me around.

I started having nightmares about the massiveness of His size. I was constantly having dreams where I saw God so big and tall that I could never see high enough to look in His face.

I am puzzled, even in my adult years, whenever I have had that same dream that it was always the chest area that shielded His face. His chest area was so big that I could never see around or over it. I was never able to see His face.

The indentations of those early experiences are still fresh in my mind. When Dad tried to console me in regard to the visions I had of the strangulation of the goats, he opened the Bible to the first book of 1 Samuel, chapter 3. He read the story of God speaking to Samuel though a child. He also read the story of King Jehoshaphat and how he became king at age eight. He told me that I was not too young for God to speak to me and to show me His secrets.

I developed a strong desire to see more of the realities of those stories that my parents had taught me. This desire slowly erased my fears because I realized that God was not following me around just to watch me or to scrutinize or penalize me.

He was not trying to bring us to an ending of destruction either. But, for the most part, He wanted to overshadow and protect us with His unfailing love. Papa gave me assignments from the Bible. It was a joy again for me to be able to read my favorite stories. One such story, which Father assigned, was taken from St. Mark 10:46. In this story, I read about a blind man whom Jesus healed.

I did not go blind as the doctor had predicted. This great, powerful God of whom I was afraid, who loved me so tenderly, restored my sight completely. Shortly after my recovery from the eye problems, I fell sick again.

With a severe fever, I had a series of convulsions. Mother took me again to the doctor. He told her that this condition was a slow attack of seizures. He went on to further inform her of how alert she would have to be around me, because I could fall off a cliff, out of a tree, or into the fire or water. This reminded me also of the story I read in Mark 9:21–23.

In this story, we read how Jesus healed the epileptic boy who sometimes fell into the fire and sometimes into the water. His father brought him to the disciples of Jesus for them to heal him, but they could not.

Mother must have prayed through again because since that time I have had no attacks from the spirit of epilepsy. By this time, I was beginning to understand my mother's attitude toward sickness that came against any of her family members. Mother fasted and prayed constantly.

In this posture, she was assured that her faith was in good standing with the God of the word. Her spiritual man remained constantly in the presence of the Most Holy One. Living in the presence of God is the most assured way of having our prayers answered. I was a very close observer of my mother.

She walked circumspectly; she was a holy woman of God, and she hesitated not to correct anyone she thought to be doing or saying the wrong things. My father knew that and so did everyone around her to whom she ministered in prayer. Who would not want to walk like she walked with God?

The apostle Paul instructs us to "walk circumspectly, not as fools but as wise; redeeming the time for the days are evil" (Ephesians 5:15–16). Mother not only knew that, but she lived that until she became the object of this lesson.

Mom and Dad warned us children about the friends we kept. They also told us that we were not better than other children but that our training was different from theirs. We tried hard to obey in all things but failed miserably.

One Sunday afternoon, after we returned home from church, we had dinner together as we did other times. As children, we went outside of the house to play. We created our own games, and we sometimes got very loud. This kind of behavior was totally unacceptable to my parents, especially on the Lord's Day.

Our behavior on the Lord's Day should supersede that of all the other days of the week. She said, "God is looking down on us with His great big eyes that can see everything."

We had gone beyond the border of our playing range one Sunday evening onto a neighbor's land. This was permissible by the owners of the land, but it became a violation against my parents' orders. Father called us all inside the house. After the reprimand, he chided me more severely because I was the oldest boy, and he gave me one of his unresolvable problems to do.

He told me that because I failed to take charge and to carry out the orders that he had implemented, I was grounded for the rest of the afternoon. My punishment was to read the Bible from Genesis to Revelation. He said, "When you are finished, you *may* go outside," with an emphasis on the "may."

I accepted the challenge but failed shortly thereafter. I became weary and tired after reading the first chapter of Genesis, and then I fell asleep. When I awakened from slumber, it was dark outside. Venturing outside at that time could not even be conceived in my mind. I went back to reading the Bible until it was bedtime.

SIX

MY ENCOUNTER WITH THE SAVIOR

I HAD A secret girlfriend, secret because only I know about her—or so I thought. She was a couple of years older, and she was beauty personified. I had great pleasure walking with her to and from school. We had very little playing time together at home because of the strictness of our parents.

My heart often leaped in retrospect whenever I passed her house and saw her playing in the yard. If only I could be with her, I pondered. Sometimes I walked very slowly or even stopped. Once, her dad saw me looking intently at her. He assessed the situation. With a smile on his face, he walked toward me, bent over, and made a lasting statement. I will never forget it. "What happened, Man? Do you love my daughter? If you love my daughter, you have to work hard to get her."

I did not know how to respond to that statement. The fact of the matter was, at that time, I was probably ten years old. My love never wavered though I was young. I became greatly disappointed when a relative of hers went away to live in the United Kingdom, and she went too. This sudden shock affected me greatly. Only eternity could reveal the extent of my loss.

School was full of fun and fantasies. I loved poetry. My interest was aroused for this subject when my second-grade teacher taught us a poem entitled "The Wind." Literature became my favorite subject. I liked reading poems and plays. I enjoyed writing poems and sonnets.

My love for literature must have developed over the years from reading the Psalms, Proverbs, and the Song of Solomon from the Holy Bible. I was so intrigued by the fact that a writer could say so much while using so few words.

The writings of Isaiah are very captivating as well. I cannot forget the last Wednesday night in February 1965. That night, I became born again. I publicly received the Lord into my life. The lead missionary of our church came to the island of Jamaica from a foreign country.

He and his entourage came to conduct a church conference. This was held in the western part of the island. After the ending of the festival, they dispersed to the different churches within the circuit. He, being the overseer of the entire organization, decided to visit the parish of St. Ann.

This was a remote area of the parish of St. Ann. There, they had one of the younger congregations in the circuit. This congregation was striving very, very much. Ninety percent of the congregants were young people. The series of meetings got started that Sunday and continued nightly for one week.

Many of the teenagers graciously and willingly gave their lives to the Lord. We grew rapidly in the things of the Lord. Praying together in the church and in the homes became a routine. There were about eleven of us young men who teamed up to read the Bible and to pray together.

There was a two-week revival meeting once in our church. These meetings got started on a Sunday night. Unlike other meetings, the services were not as lively as usual. This can be better described as being in a moving vehicle that had no pulling power.

The enemy, Satan, stood in the way with all his resistive power. The praise and worship services were lukewarm, and the musicians could not play correctly. It could be observed that the minister was under a heavy burden because his hope and prayers were for souls to be saved.

Seven of us young men decided to fast and pray that Tuesday. Following an all-night prayer that Monday night, we bonded ourselves together on one accord to tarry before God until we got a breakthrough. We met together on the Wednesday evening before the service began and we prayed. That night, the Spirit of God rained down in the assembly like we had never experienced before.

The singing was different. People spontaneously gave praise to the Lord, their hands raised. Shouts of "Hallelujah!" went up. We clapped our hands with great vigor, confidence, and assurance. The evidence of the presence of God, in the person of His Holy Spirit, was clearly expressed on the countenances of the people.

The pastor called for testimonies from the congregants. Like popcorn, we jumped to our feet, burning with zeal and confidence, willing to tell of the miraculous power of Jesus Christ. This brought eternal changes to our lives.

The message was delivered under great anointing. There was a great response as people went to the altar. Some made new commitments, while we believers recommitted ourselves to the Lord. The new level of worship became the order of our gathering.

We realized that prayer and fasting were the connecting lines between God and His church. The old man (sinful nature) was truly put to death in our lives as young people. The entrance of the newborn believers brought a new experience of the resurrection power of the cross to me.

SEVEN
THE PRAYER OF FAITH

SHORTLY AFTER THE revival, I became one of the victims of an epidemic that swept over the island. The medical practitioners described it as "dengue fever." This demonic attack took the lives and better health of many. Once it lays its deadening grasp on someone, the end result was either death or some serious health defects.

This dengue fever left some of its victims maimed or crippled or with mild cases of mental disturbance. In medical terminology, it was called *hysteria*. My mother's home remedies had no effect on the fever. It got so bad I experienced hallucinations. I stood up to walk but could not take a step without someone holding my hands or me holding on to a firm object.

Mother sent messages to the church informing them of my illness. That Sunday afternoon, my pastor's wife came to visit me. She reinforced my faith with the word, and then she prayed. Her prayers were so fervent that the demon of fever went instantly.

I knew without a doubt that God came into that room that Sunday afternoon. Shortly after she prayed, I was able to walk out of the room and into the adjacent room.

Before the week was over, I could walk to my farm. I was still physically weak, but I was determined to involve myself in the process of my breakthrough. When I got to the field, I looked up to the sky. I felt as if everything was taller and was falling down on me.

The very ground under my feet felt unstable. Without hesitation, I returned home. I did not accept defeat; however, I did go back to my bed. The next day, I returned to the field like a fighting soldier recuperating from minor wounds. I was able to eat my meals normally.

In the midst of my dilemmas, I still meditated on the word of God. The scripture the reverend ministered from came alive in my spirit that night I gave my life to the Lord. This was taken from Isaiah 53:3–6:

> He is despised and rejected by men; a man of sorrows, and acquainted with grief: and we hid as if our faces from Him; He was despised, and we esteemed Him not. Surely, He hath born our griefs, and carried our sorrows: yet we did esteem Him not. Surely He hath borne our griefs, and carried our sorrows: yet we did esteem Him stricken, smitten of God, and afflicted.
>
> But He was wounded for our transgressions, He was bruised for our iniquities: the chastisement of our peace was upon Him; and with His stripes we are healed.
>
> All we like sheep have gone astray; we have turned everyone to his own way; and the Lord hath laid on Him the iniquity of us all.

God truly hears and answers the prayers of His saints. We do get positive results from Him when we pray according to His will. He told us, "If my people, which are called by my name, shall humble themselves and pray and seek my face, and turn from their wicked ways; then will I hear from heaven, and will forgive their sins and heal their land. Now mine eyes shall be opened, and my ears attend unto the prayer that is made in this place" (2 Chronicles 7:14–15).

These verses of scripture are foundational to the Christian faith. They are the fundamentals of my faith and of my existence today. They are truth, and they are life. They breathed, they produced, and they brought forth abundantly. They have been sown in fertile ground, and the result is fruitful.

The night after the Lord wrought the work of transformation in my heart, I did not know how I would be able to deal with it. I came to realize that it was actually easier than I had thought it would be. I began to understand the reality and the result of my pursuit.

I did find the God I sought, or rather, He sought and found me. Job said, "He knows the way I take." I went to bed that night a new man. I awoke the following morning literally seeing things differently. The sun seemed to have shone brighter than before.

The trees looked different. The wild birds were of greater value to me. I even looked at the landscape as fine art. I looked at them with a new perspective. I did not know altogether what had happened, but I knew it was an unmistaken, unavoidable, and undoubted experience.

The most Holy had embodied Himself into sinful flesh one more time. And glory be to God, this was my time. I felt a peace that I knew not before. It brought completeness to my hungry heart and desires more than any other experience I have ever had.

I cried though I had no sorrow. I wondered, yet there was no lament. I could not eat, yet I felt no hunger. I was thrilled to know I had finally obtained the very thing I sought after, when as yet, I knew it not. All my confusions were washed away. My immeasurable journey had ended abruptly.

The storm of uncertainty had ceased, because the Holy Spirit had brought me into His sanctuary and placed this banner of love over me. My father was the first of the household to know of my new experience. We went to the field together, as we often did.

We were at work preparing the ground to plant our annual crops. He noticed that I stayed on the job more consistently than I had before. I became very reserved but not angry. In my pondering, my eyes became watery. When I took a break, I did not go to hunt birds or to play around as usual; instead, I went behind the cluster of the yam vines, knelt down, and prayed.

Jesus, who became my newfound Savior, met with me there. The joy I felt brought tears to my eyes. Papa noticed the distinctive changes in my demeanor, and he asked, "Are you all right, Man?"

"Yes, sir," I replied.

The conversation did not extend beyond that point. It was obvious that something had happened to me. My new experience was not something I was ready to talk about.

It was now time to prepare the lunch, so he went himself and did the cooking. After he called me to the eating place, Dad and I sat down to eat. I felt as if my appetite had evaporated so I could not eat. There was such joy bubbling up inside of me that it took away my appetite for food. I left the food and went to my scheduled spot to pray again.

Weeks went by, but my new conversion did not relinquish. Instead, I kept on growing in the faith and producing obvious changes in my demeanor. Although I was very shy, I found enough courage to testify of my experience of sins forgiven. My pastor counseled me into getting baptized. He said this was a stronger testimony to the world that I had decided to turn away from a life of sin and turn to Jesus Christ, who would produce a life of righteousness in me.

Baptismal time came during the period of time when the whole island was experiencing a severe drought. The church had a newly built pool, but there had been no rainfall for a long, long time. Therefore, the baptismal service was canceled approximately three times before it could be convened.

The local pastor arranged a prayer meeting at which time we prayed for rainfall. Not only did we need water for the pool, but farmers were losing their livestock and crops because of the severity of the drought. The meteorologist predicted that the drought would continue until October.

We were in the first week of May 1965. The church prayed island-wide, the heavens opened up to us, and God sent us rain in abundance. There was so much rain in the month of May that it was disastrous. There were mudslides in some areas. Houses were washed away, and animals drowned.

About May 9, we were able to have the baptismal service. The new concrete pool was overflowing with crystal-clear water. When the overseer stepped into the pool, the water overflowed in an admirable and glorious manner.

Of the four candidates to be baptized, three of us were young men. The first candidate to be immersed was a six-foot-two-inch-tall young man. He walked into the pool. He was as tall as the reverend. He took the first plunge. As soon as he came up out of the water, the congregation, families, friends, and well-wishers echoed the song,

Down at the cross where my Savior died.

Down where for cleansing from sin I cried. There at the cross

Where He took me in.

Glory to His name.

People were standing around. Some climbed into trees nearby, while others climbed the stone wall along the church property. I was the second candidate to step into the watery grave. I was asked to give my testimony. My very dear father was there to hear me for the first time testifying openly and in public.

They all raised their hands and praised God for saving us young people. I grew stronger and stronger in love with my newfound Savior, Jesus Christ. I love to read His words and pray. It was a routine to roll off my bed onto my knees in the mornings. The soles of my feet would never go outdoors before I prayed. This became my daily food.

As I grew in the faith, the Lord kept pouring immeasurable blessings upon me. My attitude toward others changed noticeably. My demeanor changed. I even treated the animals of other owners better than I had before.

People who were my senior began to show me higher regard, respect, and honor. They referred to me as Mr. Dixon, or Doctor Dixon.

Such accolades did not come cheaply. These came as a result of strenuous self-sacrifices, such as constant reading of the word of God, much fasting, and many prayers. No one wants to take my place there because it is not friendly to be alone when friendship is available.

I realized I could build an altar to God and offer myself as a living sacrifice to Him any time and any place, and it became an acceptable challenge. This was the altar that the apostle Paul wrote about in Romans 12:1–2:

> I beseech you therefore, brethren, by the mercies of God, that ye present your bodies a living sacrifice, holy, acceptable unto God, which is your reasonable service. And be not conformed to this world: but be ye transformed by the renewing of your mind that ye may prove what is that good, and acceptable, and perfect will of God.

Whenever I go to the Lord in prayer, I find that He is there already waiting on me. He has never disappointed me once. He always floods my soul with unexplainable joys. It is exactly as these words go. These words somehow provide just a taste of such experiences:

Joys are flowing like a river, since the comforter has come.

He abides with us forever Makes the trusting heart His home

Blessed quietness, Holy quietness, blest assurance in my soul!

On the stormy sea, Jesus speaks peace to me, and the billows cease to roll.

Will I be able to fully explain the depth of joy that I have found in Christ Jesus, my Savior? Not in this lifetime. I don't think. It is truly amazing, unfathomable; it is unexplainable, and it is indeed life-changing!

In this new experience, I became stronger, wiser, and more tolerant. I personally established a special time of month when I would take off from work to fast and pray. Sundays were my regular fast day, but that time was not as conducive. I chose a spot where I could be as private as possible, and there established an altar before the Lord.

The church held a community fast every first Monday of the month. I retired to my secluded spot, where it was peaceful and very quiet, every second Monday of the month, to meet with my Lord. This particular spot was on the very top of a hill, which we called "Big Hill."

This was a dividing factor between two districts called Upper and Lower Caledonia.

I was born, raised, and lived in the upper region. Our little home was approximately five hundred feet up from the foot of the hill on the easterly side.

Just below our little house, my father grew coffee, bananas, and citrus fruits. Large cedar and avocado trees grew among the fruit trees, which blanketed our little house. These trees formed a canopy for my secret trail, which led to my sanctuary on top of Big Hill.

At the edge of the plantation, there was a long stretch of solid rock located between our home and that of one of my mother's uncles. This rock was about two hundred feet long and about fifteen feet high, at the highest point. This rock formed the foot of Big Hill.

Some trees grew on top of it and up to the edge. Those trees sent roots down on the side or face of the rock to pull the nutrients from the rich, fertile earth below. The roots made climbing the rock much easier. I chose a spot that was not observable to passersby and less treacherous for me to climb. It so happened that this was the highest point of the rock.

I would pull some (in our terminology, whist) wild slip and tie my sack with my Bible and songbook to it. This was known as a burlap bag. I attached one end to my pant loop and the other to the bag. Reaching the top of the rock, I then pulled my sack up with my sword and shield.

I climbed up Big Hill, sometimes jumping from one rock to the other. It was approximately 2,500 feet up to the top. Some parts of Big Hill had no earth to reinforce the trees to grow so my only disguises were the whitish-gray rocks protruding upward. There I had some enjoyable admiration for the rocks, which appeared to be packed in order, forming orderly contours.

Once at the top of Big Hill where there was a healthy clump of trees and shrubs, I rested before I started praying. Underneath these trees lay a bed of soft, dry leaves, twigs, and fallen limbs. I chose a special spot from which I would clear my desired spot. I spread out my burlap bag like a magic blanket and there offered myself to the Lord.

That place had become my sanctuary. Only the birds were my visitors. My intrusion quickly drove them away when I was spotted. It was always a cool and comfortable place to meditate on the things that my soul longed for.

Occasionally a calm breeze would pass through leaving the air fresh and relaxing. This became my secret prayer chamber where I could shut the world out and be enclosed with my newfound friend, my kinsman and redeemer. That was my place of sacredness, where heaven touched earth and the Holy One met the unholy.

EIGHT
MY MENTOR

MY NUMBER-ONE EARTHLY mentor died when I was at the age of nineteen. My mother was very limited in the knowledge of earthly wealth. Based upon my research, I soon too realized that one can be limited in life without proper resources. Limitation can hold one trapped in a mental box. We have to learn to think outside of that box.

Staying in that box can be devastating and life-threatening. My two friends' father encouraged me to be aware of my potential and God-given talents. He was a successful farmer and a devout man. He was a deacon in the Baptist church and very prominent in society. He was a man of great wisdom and counsel.

I grew to love, honor, and appreciate him for his insights into my life path. He showed me the path of independence and self-reliance. He recognized the abilities that God had deposited in me. He uplifted my spirit and confirmed that the Lord was with me. He also told me that whatever I wanted to become, I could be; I need only to always put God first in everything I did.

These became my watchwords. I continued to attend the church in my district. Based on visions I had had, I knew that I would not be there forever. I had seen myself in places I never knew. I kept fasting and praying about my future in God and in the world of economics. I realized that I could be the biggest hindrance to my progress.

I became more consistent and determined to create a life for myself that my parents did not know. Shortly thereafter, things began to change for the better.

NINE
THE HOLY SPIRIT EXPLAINED

THE CHURCH IN which I got saved never taught the baptism of the Holy Ghost. They taught sanctification to be the second definite work of the Holy Spirit in our lives after repentance.

Speaking in tongues was not taught to be of any importance. But in my understanding and experience of Acts 2, such teaching fell short of the full revelation of the gospel of the Lord Jesus Christ and the kingdom of God. I came to realize that there was a higher level of experience in Christ that was bound up in the third person of the trinity.

This revelation can only be taught by one who has obtained that experience. I was saved for more than five years before I came into the deeper understanding of the work of the Holy Spirit in the church. There was always a hunger and a thirst, a longing and a yearning for something else deep down inside my inner being.

There was an unfulfilled vacuum in my life, a sense of powerlessness that I could not explain. There was something that made my mother shout; it made her happy and joyful, even in the midst of lack. This put heat in her prayers and caused them to burn in my heart.

This was what I longed for. I came close to having this glorious experience on Big Hill.

It was Monday afternoon. I had spent the day with the Lord upon Big Hill. I was nearing the end of my prayer time when I would descend the hill. I was in my final prayer. Suddenly, I had an unexplainable experience. I knew that no other human being was there with me, but I felt the presence of someone else.

With my eyes closed, I continued to pray. I was doubtful that I was there alone. My speech left me, I felt a chill all over my body. My head felt like it was of an unusual size. My eyes closed tightly, and my mouth opened with a silent praise. A battle began to be waged in my mind.

Should I open my eyes to see if someone was standing there watching me? But then a quick thought rushed through my mind. *If someone came that close, I would have heard footsteps.* Questions began to flood my mind: *Should I open my eyes? And if I open my eyes, what will I see?*

I remembered reading in scriptures where angelic beings appeared to men like Abraham and Moses and the prophet Isaiah also. All of them reacted the same way: they were scared out of their wits. *What if there is an angel?* I wondered. *What would be the angel's form, shape, or appearance? How many of them would I see?*

My flesh man intervened, and I started to create answers for my own thoughts. I reasoned that it could be a mongoose, a dog, or just a large bird perched on a branch above my head. In my spirit, I knew that I had had a heavenly visitation. I knew that I could not deal with these experiences by myself.

I wanted to call my mother because I believed she would understand, but she could not hear me from that distance. If I screamed, someone else might have heard me. Being the shy and reserved individual I was, I pondered in my heart, and then I rested in the overcoming thoughts that God must have sent His angels to let me know that He had heard my prayers.

I finally opened my eyes, and with intense trembling, I rose to my feet. My knees were uncooperative. My hands volunteered to aid my feet. It was by far a greater task to descend the mountain at that time than it had been for me to ascend it. It must be that the Lord had sent His angels who carried me to safety.

Those months I spent with the Lord on Big Hill had escalated my soul to the highest altitudes in the Spirit. There were moments when the unseen God gave me plain revelations of Himself as He did for whoever would trust and obey Him in ancient times.

I did not see Him in natural form, but every trace of doubt about Him coming close to His children was erased. I knew that He was real. That day, I felt as if a flame was burning inside of me. I did not have the experience of the baptism of the Holy Spirit at that time.

I had no knowledge, no understanding as to what the baptism of the Holy Spirit was all about. I was naive to this life-changing experience. It is after the baptism into the Holy Spirit that He brings forth His fertilizing power in the barrenness of human life. It is then that the resurrecting power of the Holy Spirit comes into the deadness of the human's immortal soul.

These moments bring revelation of dying to one's flesh and transform us into the life of the Spirit. It is in these moments of transformation that the believer is brought to a state of being a new creation. Old things have passed away, and a newness of life has begun.

The fire on the altar will burn away all the dross and give way for the heavenly dove to settle on you. Heaven rejoices in those highly productive moments, because the ultimate purpose of the cross of Jesus has been brought into an unavoidable view.

It is then that one is brought from death to life. Thus, the life of Christ has permeated your being. Now you can say, "I am crucified with Christ; nevertheless, I live, yet not I, but the Christ that lives in me: and the life which I now live in the flesh, I live by the faith of the son of God, who loved me: and gave Himself for me" (Galatians 2:20).

These experiences are sequential marks, which are to aid or lead us on our journey into knowing and living in the third dimension of God's grace. This truly is a taste of the power of the world that is to come. For many years, I kept on believing that being sanctified was the baptism of the Holy Ghost.

To be sanctified is to be set aside for service. But to be filled with the Holy Ghost is to be prepared for service. Before Jesus's ascension, He told His disciples that He would pray to the Father and the Father would send us, the church, another comforter.

John, the disciple of Jesus, wrote in John 14:15–17,

If ye love me, keep my commandments.

> And I will pray the Father, and He shall give you another comforter, that He may abide with you forever;
> Even the Spirit of truth; whom the world cannot receive, because it seeth Him not, neither knoweth Him: but ye knoweth Him; for He dwelleth with you, and shall be in you.

Jesus also said to them, "And, behold, I send the promise of my father upon you: but tarry ye in the city of Jerusalem, until ye be endued with power from on high" (Luke 24:49).

This great promise was prophesied by the prophet Joel. "And it shall come to pass afterward, that I will pour out my spirit upon all flesh; and your sons and your daughters shall prophesy, your old men shall dream dreams, your young men shall see vision. And also upon the servants and upon the handmaids in those days will I pour out my Spirit."

Historians said that Joel's prophecy came eight hundred years before its fulfillment on the day of Pentecost. This was the promise that Jesus Christ reiterated to His disciples as shown here. Let's go to the book of

Acts and see what took place on that day when the church came together on one accord.

> And when the day of Pentecost was fully come. They were in one accord in one place. And suddenly there came a sound from heaven as of a rushing mighty wind, and it filled all the house where they were sitting.
>
> And there appeared unto them cloven tongues like as of fire, and it sat upon each of them. And they were all filled with the Holy Ghost, and began to speak with other tongues, as the Spirit gave them utterance. (Acts 2:1–4)

After the believers received the promise from the Father, Peter preached his first Holy-Ghost-anointed sermon and won over three thousand souls to the kingdom of God. The reason some of us cannot win a soul is because we are just set apart to serve.

We need to get the infilling, the indwelling, and the anointing of the mighty Holy Spirit. It is He who will empower us to fulfil the assignment from our Father, who is in heaven.

To tarry is to wait patiently. The early church waited for the promise. The result of their patient waiting was the coming to pass of the divine promise from the Father.

God is the God of covenant. He made them, and He keeps them. We read in Peter's expository epistle: "The Lord is not slack concerning His promise, as some men count slackness; but is longsuffering to us-ward, not willing that any should perish, but that all should come to repentance" (2 Peter 3:9).

The eternal Father made the promise; He keeps the promise! He knew that no one would be able to withstand the evil forces of darkness in the world without supernatural help from heaven.

It is factual that from ancient times whenever servants of God have encountered opposing forces beyond their control, they have cried out to

Him and He has dispatched angels to their aid. The prophet Daniel was confronted with opposition to his faith in God while he was in Babylonian captivity.

He was told not to petition any other God besides the king, Nebuchadnezzar. This event came after he was appointed head president over the princes of Babylon. We read in chapter 6:3, "Then this Daniel was preferred above the presidents and princes, because an excellent spirit was found in him; and the King thought to set him over the whole realm."

Out of jealousy for the newly appointed position, the other presidents and princes sought to dethrone Daniel by plotting a destructive scheme against him. Because there was found an excellent Spirit in him, they hated him. The devil knows who we are, and he will always seek to undermine us.

They watched him praying three times per day within the time limit in which no petition should have been made to any other god but King Nebuchadnezzar. Daniel knew that he was in trouble since the day of his appointment.

This drove him into more intense prayers. He knew that mediocre prayer would not avail. Hit-and-miss prayer was not going to bring the protection he needed. Therefore, he began to pray three times a day. Daniel decided that if he was ever going to prove to his enemies that indeed his faith in the Most High God was intact, he had to pray openly and without fear.

We read in verse four of chapter six, "Then the presidents and Princes sought to find occasion against Daniel concerning the Kingdom; but they could find none occasion nor fault; forasmuch as he was faithful, neither was there any error or fault found in him."

Daniel's indictment came when he was found guilty of petitioning his God contrary to the king's decree. His sentence was death by being fed to the hungry lions. Daniel's prayers rose up as a memorial before God.

And in answering him, God dispatched His angels another time on his behalf, sending him deliverance.

Surviving the crushing jaws and paws of the fierce, angry, and hungry lions, Daniel shouted with a voice of victory, as the very anxious king peered down the dark chute into the den of lions inquiring, "Is your God able to deliver you?"

"O King, live forever. My God hast sent His angel, and hath shut the lion's mouths …" (Daniel 6:21–22).

Here we can see that the baptism, the filling and the indwelling of the excellent spirit, has brought deliverance to the servant of God. So we see that when we call on His name, He answers with unexplainable miracles.

In the story of Hannah also, she was gripped by the jaws of a demeaning monster out of whose grasp her husband could not pray her release. The priest could not pray her release. Hannah, therefore, prayed unto to God, by herself, and He provided that excellent Spirit. Her answer came in a package of fertility.

She laid hold on the altar, and she cried unto God. He heard the cry of a desperate, barren woman. This was a woman who was disdained and ridiculed by her peers. There probably were times when she was embarrassed to go out of her house.

She took her burden to the Lord, and she left it there. She left her package of troubles there and went home free from cares and worry. She went home with an assurance that God had answered her prayer. Hannah believed God; therefore, she received the petition that she put before the Lord.

We read, "… when the time was come about after Hanna had conceived, that she bear a son, and called him Samuel, saying, because I have asked him of the Lord" (1 Samuel 1:20). God came through for His desperate child because He has committed Himself to answer the prayers of His children.

We are instructed by the writer of Hebrews 10:22–23, "Let us draw near with a true heart in full assurance of faith, having our hearts sprinkled from an evil conscience, and our bodies washed with pure water. Let us hold fast the profession of our faith without wavering; (for He is faithful that promise)."

TEN
MY PROTECTIVE SHIELD

I HAD A dream once. I saw myself standing in front of a giant who was notorious because of his championship. He boasted of his great strength and accomplishments. His intentions were to intimidate me. I refused to be intimidated by him because of the confidence that I had and demonstrated in my champion whose name was Jesus Christ.

This self-exalted champion began to diminish as I kept repeating the power of my champion defender. When he first approached me, he almost intimidated me. He was so tall that from his feet to his knees equaled my entire height.

Jesus the Christ is our true, all-time, undisputed champion. He defeated Lucifer when He hung on the cross. Satan ruled over the souls of men from the time of Adam and Eve up to the time of Jesus's crucifixion.

He ruled with tyranny over God's creation. The devil set himself up as a slave master and did whatsoever he pleased. No one could defy him. He slaughtered whomever he would. The word *mercy* had no place in his kingdom.

No human had the power to oppose him; no one could conquer him. He did whatever he wanted because he was in charge of the earth. But when Jesus the Christ came to establish His kingdom, Satan's self-established rule began to unravel.

The devil plotted and schemed, but none of his tricks could prevail for him. Satan was, is, and always will be a defeated foe. He has nothing, and he owns nothing. We read in Psalm 24:1–2, "The earth is the Lord's, and the fullness thereof; the world, and they that dwell therein. For He hath founded it upon the seas, and established it upon the floods." The intruder has been captured and shall be discarded by our champion, the Lord Jesus Christ. That enemy of our souls has worn out the saints of the Most High God, but our Lord and Savior, Jesus Christ, has renewed strength.

He truly revives our souls and makes us live in Him. Because his final sentence has not yet been handed down, Satan is still roaming the earth, seeking whom he may devour. When I look back and see the treacherous path I had to walk through because of the devil, I realize that the grace of God is truly sufficient.

Through those experiences, I found out that Satan had lost his hold on me. I started to live in Christ and live victoriously. I started to live the experiences taught by Jesus in Mark 16. The chain that the devil used to bind me was broken forever.

Now I can help others to rid themselves of Satan's bondage. The two main tools that the Holy Spirit gave me to use were the blood and the name of Jesus. The devil came out against me another time. I moved to live in the corporate area, which is the capital city.

I was employed and trained to be a bus conductor. My training period took half of the expected time, so my employers had me working by myself. I was assigned the second to the oldest bus in the fleet. I was working on the very least busy shift.

My rookie days were very successful. This impressed my employer greatly but infuriated my coworkers and fellow conductors in other companies sharing the same bus route. They became very indignant and bitter against me.

I was spoken about rather disparagingly, and they further plotted my assassination. Their fury was caused by my honesty and productivity. Because of their dishonesty, I became a star or a rose among the thorns.

The illumination of my Christian practices exposed their deception. A clear revelation of underhandedness illuminated all the owners of the four private bus companies that shared the route.

This news spread like wildfire. Many of these employees claimed to be Christians and so were trusted by their employers. When their bosses discovered their unscrupulous acts, they were chided harshly, and some were fired.

I was a trusted employee, shunned by my coworkers and hated by the workers from the affiliated companies. I became a thorn in their sides. There were rules laid out by the companies that were to encourage harmony, honesty, and productivity.

Some of the rules were that we had one free meal per day, no alcoholic beverages were allowed on the job, and the drivers were to notify the conductor of that particular bus if the bus became disabled.

I was working the evening shift, which started at two o'clock and ended at eight in the evening. We stopped at our regular spot for dinner. Upon entering the restaurant, both the driver and I ordered our meals. He was an older gentleman. With respect for him, I gave the privilege to him to use the restroom first.

He refused and became very adamant. After much persuasion to no avail, I went. The time for my relief had elapsed by then, and I returned to the table. My meal was already placed on the table with him sitting there.

Just as soon as he saw me coming toward the table, he got up in haste, and off to the restroom he went. I sat, blessed my food, and ate. He decided he was not eating.

Approximately thirty minutes after eating, I developed a stomachache and became nauseated. I started feeling weak on the way to the bus depot. I felt as if I was in a state of mild delirium, which was accompanied by serious regurgitation.

This lasted about an hour. I was experiencing vertigo (dizziness). My speech was affected, and my knees were giving way to the angel of death. I was forced to abandon my second trip for the day. I informed the driver about my illness, and he sent word to my employer about my emergency condition.

One of the partners came immediately to inquire about my well-being and to collect the money. Thinking it was just a mild stomachache, he suggested I rest for the night and have the doctor check me the following day if the illness persisted.

The following day, I was even more helpless. My roommates had to help me to and from the bathroom. My condition got increasingly worse by the hour. All objects to me were unstable. I informed them of my condition, and all three of them got together and prayed over me.

As young Christian men in the country, all night tarrying and praying together became our lifestyle. Prayer and the studying of the word became our daily bread. I later found out I had been poisoned in the meal I had at the restaurant.

After praying, I began to experience a speedy recovery, and three days later, I was back on the job. I was still weak in my body, but I continued exercising my faith in God.

In my spirit, I began investigating the whole scenario. Multiple questions rushed through my mind. The what, the who, and the why questions terrified me. What could cause me to be sick in the first place? The illness was severe. I lost some weight in three days.

My friends and neighbors asked, "What really happened to you?"

"You look drugged," they all concluded.

After all the unanswered questions and the prayers of the brethren, which were certainly answered, I dismissed everything from my mind.

The devil does not give up as quickly as we Christians do. He is persistent, although he knows that he is already defeated. Satan brought another plot; this was to terminate me from the job and the world.

After I got well, I returned to my job.

After leaving the bus stand one evening about six o'clock, approximately forty minutes into the second and final trip for the day, I noticed that the bus came to a standstill while I was busy collecting the fares from the passengers. They began to be agitated.

I investigated the matter. A few of the passengers started to get off the bus in great haste. One of the patrons shouted in Jamaican colloquial, "A wha kind a conducta dis a collect man money aun no si dat de bus bruck dung?" This sent a strong demand to my attention.

I questioned, "What did you say?"

The remaining passengers on the bus demanded that I give them back their fares. I went to inquire of the driver what was the matter. His answer was that he did not know what went wrong with the bus.

I turned around to attend to the remaining passengers, only to find out that there were some bandits among them who demanded I refund them their money.

There were also some young boys and young men (outlaws) hanging around the sides of the bus. As I observed the situation, I saw one of them with an open ratchet knife in his right hand. He yelled out to me in his street language, "Hai yu, misa conducta, gi mi mi money now."

These guys occasionally rode on the sides of the buses because they did not want to pay their fares. At his demand for a refund, I boldly told him that if he was on the bus, he should come inside with his ticket, and then I would refund him.

This further infuriated him. As soon as I turned my back to him and continued to collect tickets and return the fares, I heard a loud bang on the window glass, which was partially broken out.

I turned to see what had happened. I saw him with his right hand stretched out, his blood dripping and the knife in the same hand. Moments flew by, and there he was standing in front of me inside the bus. I was amazed.

In his anger and embarrassment—he was the gang leader—he shouted at me with the bleeding hand gripping the knife, blaming me for causing his hand to be cut. I returned the question, "I caused your hand to be cut?"

I did not wait for an answer from him. The Holy Spirit directed my attention to the little emergency door by the steering wheel. Apparently, when the driver made his escape, he left it open. I jumped over the engine, which created a partition between the driver and the one passenger seat on the left.

In all of this scenario, I was astonished, because the person who gave the news flash about the bus's disablement was not a paying passenger. He was riding on the side of the bus. The danger the passenger faced with being on the bus at that particular time could be described as that of an overcrowded theater when an idler shouted, "Fire!" or of finding oneself in the middle of a dogfight.

Everyone was aware that someone was in serious danger. Some took their belongings and fled the scene by foot. Others pulled together, demanding their money be returned. I was caught in the middle of it all. I became the broader target. Only the angels of the living God could allow me to escape such terror.

For me to make my escape, I would have to pass the angry, frightened, and ignorant mob. There were three distinct groups of people comprising this mob. There were those who were demanding what was theirs. Another group wanted whatever they could get. The third group was assigned as angels of death.

They wanted my life. They were there for my blood. I realized that when one of those outlaws shouted at me from outside the bus, he was demanding that I return his money, knowing that he had never paid a fare. I remember the appearance of the weapon as if it were yesterday.

It was a bone-handle ratchet knife with a curved end, painted in a rich wine color. It had an eight-inch pointed blade. The blade was riveted into the handle with a spring. It had a ring located between the blade and the handle.

The user of the knife would insert his index finger into the ring and then reinforce the handle while pulling back on the ring. The blade would fly open with a force, ready for action.

While the operator pulled back on the spring, he flashed the knife with his hands for a quick release. That action prepared him for instant plunging of the blade into his victim.

While I was yet looking at him, he looked up and saw me looking at him. He shouted at me in patois, "Aye, you, Mister Conducta, yuh se weh yuh mek mi han cut! I want back mi monie now!"

I then replied, "I let you cut your hand? If you were on the bus, come inside with your ticket, and I will refund your money."

He gave me no answer, but I could see the vengeance in his eyes. If the windows in the bus were closed, he could not have gotten so far as to try stabbing at me. The rounded Plexiglas window unfortunately had been broken by the vandals.

Before I could make my escape from the bus, he and his accomplices stormed inside the bus, demanding money. The driver of the bus had already made his escape, leaving me to face the mob totally uniformed.

He had exited the bus through a small hatch door beside his seat, designed only for drivers. This was impossible for someone to use it if not seated at the driver's seat because the steering wheel was in the way.

I sensed that I was in big trouble. Only the Most High Himself could have orchestrated my escape route. I was blocked from the front door by the bandits. They somehow knew I could not go to the emergency door.

With no time to process my thoughts I quickly aimed for the steering wheel. In an impulsive acrobatic motion, I grabbed the wheel and spun around. In a breech position, I landed feetfirst on the pavement.

It was unbelievable to imagine my bones were still intact. Had I landed a few inches forward through the momentum of my body weight, I would have been carried into the path of a passing vehicle. I felt like a man who was running from a lion and a bear caught him. In such despair, I stood there trying to regain my composure.

The car passed by with such speed, I could have been hit, but my assigned angel intervened. Jehovah God in His infinite mercy and grace placed His protective shield around me. All praises be to Him.

Every time I reminisce on His omnipresence and omnipotence, I am humbled all the more. Satan might have set up his roadblocks, but the almighty Yahweh had already planned ahead of him every time. When I landed on the pavement with my back pressed up against the front wheel of the bus, the gang members, like vultures, descended upon me. They formed a semicircle around me.

I had barely regained my composure before they began to strip me of the money I had on me. Satan always worked with backups, but my Almighty Jehovah prevailed every single time.

There were nine of them gathered around me, each one with a knife clenched in his fist. Divine intervention prevailed another time. Some helped themselves to some of the cash, while others had their lips tightly closed and eyes wandering around.

Had it not been that some of them secured the cash in their possession, those vultures would have swept down and sliced me like tomatoes and cucumbers. This all happened at the traffic light while it was on red.

A taxicab approached the intersection while the light was red. The driver prepared to stop when the light changed. I yelled for help, for him to stop, but he recognized what was happening and just kept on driving.

Holding to the handle of the rear door, I ran alongside the car, hoping he would stop, but he never did. Determined to make my escape, I kept on running and holding on until I was out of breath.

When I did let go, I realized I had run holding onto the cab far away from my assailants and the crowd. I imagined that they must have thought I had eventually gotten into the taxi. My Lord and Savior, Jesus Christ, intervened for me that night.

The prophet Isaiah prophesied that "No weapon that is formed against thee shall prosper; and every tongue that shall rise against thee in judgment thou shall condemn. This is the heritage of the servant of the Lord, and their righteousness is of me, saith the Lord" (Isaiah 54:17).

The words of the Lord are true; they are "Yea and Amen. He watches over His words to perform them." God has promised to answer our prayers when we pray in faith believing. The things that we are in need of and ask for shall be granted to us.

God said to Israel by the mouth of the prophet Jeremiah,

> For I know the thoughts I think towards you saith the Lord, thoughts of peace and not of evil, to give you an expected end. Then shall he call upon me, and ye shall go and pray unto me, and I will hearken unto you. And you shall seek and find me, when you search for me with all your heart. And I will be found of you, said the Lord. And I will turn away your captivity. (Jeremiah 29:11–14)

ELEVEN
COMING TO AMERICA

IT IS TOTALLY impossible for God (Jehovah) to lie. We read in 2 Peter 3:9, "The Lord is not slack concerning His promises, as some men count slackness; but He is longsuffering to us ward, not willing that any should perish, but that all should come to repentance."

He also mentioned in Isaiah 46:11b: "Yea, have I spoken it, I will also bring it to pass; I have purposed it, I will do it." John wrote, "Beloved, I wish above all things that thou should prosper and be in health, even as thy soul prospers" (3 John 1:2).

As a young believer with adverse financial needs, I thought that it was proper for me to fast and pray to God for a financial blessing. At that time, my faith and confidence in Jehovah God were still in the immature stage, like a newborn baby's.

I was very eager to find out if God would answer my prayers as well as He did my mother's. I had only the accomplishments of my mother and the accounts that I read in the Bible to stand on. My faith's foundation was just beginning to be laid. I thought my mother had laid a strong enough foundation; therefore, I went ahead and built on it.

I came to find out that I could lay my own. I needed to establish my own relationship with my creator, just like anyone else. This is the way that God designed it to be. He wants me to know Him in a personal way, a way that I could relate to Him as Father and Son. God should never be taken for granted.

It is mandatory that we humble ourselves before Him and that we remain in the same posture in His presence. Once I established and built that relationship, nothing would be impossible unto me. I also found out that the Father had already laid the foundation, and all I had to do was to build.

"For other foundations can no man lay than that is laid which is Jesus Christ" (1 Corinthians 3:11). Jesus said in St. John 15:16, "Ye have not chosen me, but I have chosen you, and ordained you, that ye should go and bring forth fruit, and that your fruit should remain, that whatsoever you shall ask of the Father in my name, He shall give it to you."

I always envisioned myself traveling to the United States of America. I did not know how it would become possible. I knew no one who could sponsor me. Divine intervention set in as I remember those days going up to Big Hill to fast and pray. I sought after Him for a financial miracle.

Not knowing what to expect when He came through, I learned to trust Him. He made me to experience His love when He saved my soul. Every encounter with the enemy only taught me to know the Sovereign Lord better.

I was anxious and full of confidence. I refused to continue in my rut of environmental limitations. My parents grew us up the best way they knew how. I believed I should advance in life because of the training they gave to us children.

They had raised me to become somebody of purpose beyond their time. When I did choose the latter and relocated to the city, I was in search of improving my life in order to help someone else below my position. When I gained that employment with the bus company, I knew that was a stepping-stone to success. That was the stepping-stone of my prayers upon Big Hill.

To the Corinthian church, Paul said, "But thanks be to God, which giveth us the victory through our Lord Jesus Chris. Therefore, my beloved brethren, be ye steadfast, unmovable, always abounding in the work of the Lord, for as much as ye know that your labor is not in vain in the Lord" (1 Corinthians 15:57–58).

Migration evolved in the year 1970. This came as a surprise. With God's divine intervention, miracles began to take place. There are times in our lives when opportunities to advance our purpose come, but we sometimes take them for granted.

This taught me to welcome everything the Lord appropriated in my life. In admonishing the church in Rome, the apostle Paul wrote, "And we know that all things work together for good to them that love God, to them who are the called according to his purpose."

There are times when God brings His special people into our lives to propel us into our destiny. I also came to the realization that the common enemy was everywhere and was not limited to any one country.

The devil is a global enemy. He "came to steal, kill and to destroy" (John 10:10). Jesus was alerting the people that the truth that He preached would be challenged by the enemy. There are times when God has made provisions in fulfilling His plans for our lives, but the devil creates doubts in our minds so that we doubtfully question God.

It is in times like these that a believer needs to be able to identify the voice of the Good Shepherd from that of the liar. The devil is a schemer. He will stop at nothing to deceive the children of God. He is insanely jealous of us because what he has lost, we have gained.

When I came to America, I found out, right quickly, that the devil was here waiting for me. The battle against me only changed grounds; the fierceness and the intensity were not diminished.

He knew that if he set up his traps for me in the world, it would be difficult for him to catch me. Therefore, he sat up in the church and waited for me. Amid the initial difficulties, things appeared to be good and promising. Although the enemy changed his uniform, he fought with the same tactics.

Upon the discovery of this information, I proceeded in the battle with my usual weapon.

> (For the weapons of our warfare are not carnal, but mighty through God to the pulling down of strong holds). Casting down imaginations, and every high thing that exalteth itself against the knowledge of God, and bringing into captivity every thought to the obedience of Christ; and having in a readiness to revenge all disobedience, when your obedience is fulfilled. (2 Corinthians 10:4–6)

When we fight with these weapons that our master gave unto us, we are sure to be victorious. The blood of Jesus is a weapon. The name of Jesus is a victorious weapon. The word of God is a sure weapon. Saints, we cannot lose a single battle when we deploy these weapons by faith.

We are victorious when we exercise our faith in the word of God. The word of God is the weapon given to us to bring down strongholds. The enemy sets up his garrison at our front doors and dares us to venture out to enjoy our divine freedom.

King David and the nation of Israel were under attack by their enemies, the Philistines. The Philistines cut Israel off from their food and their water supplies. David was hiding in the cave of Adullam. Three of David's mightiest men stood up against the Philistine army and defeated them in Israel's barley fields.

Thus their food source was restored. These same three stalwarts went to see King David in the cave of Adullam. While they were in the presence of David, in his weariness, "And David the King said: And David longed, and said, Oh that one would give me drink of the water of the well of Bethlehem, which is by the gate!" (2 Samuel 23:8–39).

The armies of the Philistines at this time had set their garrison at the gate of Bethlehem. Thus they were daring King David and his army to come and take of the water. David knew of the thirst-quenching quality of that water, and so he longed after it.

As soon as the words fell from the lips of the king and registered in the ears of these anointed men, they took off running to fetch water for the king. They had no time to think of their own importance. They became consumed with the request of their king.

"... the King's business required haste" (1 Samuel 21:8c). Haste required strength. The king's business demanded quickness. To be quick, one must be energetic and alert. "Not slothful in business; fervent in spirit; serving the Lord" (Romans 12:11).

These three mighty men of valor got the job done without hesitation. Nothing could stand in front of them. Neither the size nor fierceness of the enemy's army could stop them. They knew of the power and faithfulness of the God of their fathers.

Therefore, with full confidence, they marched up to the well and commanded what belonged to them to be released unto them. These were extraordinary men. The anointing of the Holy Ghost adds the extra to the ordinary.

He makes an individual become an army to be reckoned with. It is said, "One shall chase a thousand and two shall put ten thousand to flight." King David recognized the dedication of these stalwarts.

In his evaluation of their dedication, commitment, and accomplishments, he said only the eternal God was worthy of such sacrifice. Therefore, he poured out the water on the ground before the God of the armies of Israel, who was the God of their fathers, Abraham, Isaac, and Jacob.

The lentil fields, the barley fields, and the water supply were all under the control of Israel's enemies. The fierceness of the devil will not allow him to turn away from the children of God. He wants us dead. He is seeking to cut off anyone who will praise or seek God.

The Psalmist David wrote in the 103 division of the Psalm, "Like as a father pitieth his children, so the Lord pitieth them that fear Him." This shows that whatever need we may have, our heavenly Father has long made provision for us.

Our Father knew that we would encounter the opposition brought about and enforced by the enemy of our soul. Therefore, He sent the third person of the Trinity to see to it that we not only got what He had prepared for us, but that we got it on time.

To aid us in possessing our possessions, which the Father has sent us, He sends the blessed Holy Ghost. It is He who has revealed to us that we do not have to accept defeat from the devil. He is here to help us take back what has been stolen from us.

The Holy Ghost has put a demand on the devil to let go what does not belong to him. But we must be willing to cooperate with Him. We need to go in with the Holy Ghost and demand our stuff. Abraham's nephew Lot suffered the loss of all that he had because the land where he chose to live came under siege by their enemies.

One of his servants escaped to go and tell Abraham of the deluge of his nephew. Abraham gathered his own trained men who were born in his house and went after the bandits. When he overtook them, he put a demand on them to return all that was taken, including the women and children.

Abraham knew that God was with him; therefore, he boldly demanded of the enemy to restore all that which was rightfully Lot's. Until we recognize that our heavenly Father has given us dominion over the work of His hands and move in total confidence to occupy it, we will continue to go around in circles. The enemy will continue to occupy our vineyard while we are in doubt or ignorance.

God wants us to reign over the work of His hands. The prophet Hosea disclosed this truth in chapter 4:6 of his prophecy. "My people are destroyed for lack of knowledge." When we despise knowledge, we are destined to make destructive mistakes.

The knowledge that is pertinent to our survival is nestled in the word of God. Our victories are there. Our future is there. Our place of fulfilment is written there. Moses became frustrated not sure what the next move of God was. He and the people stood still as if they were stuck in a valley of frustration.

He knew the right words to speak, but how to implement them was not clear. He tried to comfort the heart of the people, but that was not enough. He began to cry unto the Lord, who responded with these words:

> And the Lord said unto Moses, wherefore (why) criest thou unto me? Speak unto the children of Israel, that they go forward: But lift thou up thy rod, and stretch out thine handover the sea, and divide it: and the children of Israel shall go on dry ground through the midst of the sea. (Exodus 14:15–16)

God wants us to be involved in the process of our deliverance.

It takes spiritual maturity for one to be able to discern the plot of the enemy. Paul in Ephesians 6 forewarned us of the level of awareness that we should maintain in order that we will be able to combat the evil one. He wrote, "Put on the whole armor of God that you may be able to stand against the wiles of the enemy."

There was a man who became fully persuaded by the Spirit and the word of God. He was one who had ultimate respect for spiritual authority. He was grossly misled by leadership. This misleading left him bound in a matrimonial trap.

This man was introduced to and coached into marrying someone who had sold her soul to the devil, in exchange for earthly wealth and prosperity. However, the husband was completely sold out to the Lord. There were constant conflicts in the home.

Listening to his testimonies, he revealed his constant face-to-face combat with demonic forces. He told of an experience where the demonic link between his mate and the source of evil requested items of his personal belongings. They used them in their rituals.

The expressed purpose was to forcefully induct him into the cultic belief. He brought it to my attention. We fasted and prayed for three days, seeking God for this man's deliverance. The Lord intervened and miraculously brought him out. The link between the source of evil and the mate was destroyed, but it set me up as a target to the enemy.

When a saint is covered under the blood of the Lord Jesus Christ, the enemy cannot harm him or her. The enemy tried to attack me from various avenues but failed in all his attempts. Victories came because faith in God produced power for overcoming the evil one.

These forces of evil came against me with terror. I went to visit his home, but he was out. I was just about to leave when the wife told me the husband would be back shortly so I should wait. Dinner was served, and mine was placed before me. She appointed me a seat at the table. Just then, the Spirit of God spoke to me audibly. "Don't eat."

I allowed my stinking thinking to override the Spirit's warning. Thinking I was plagued by my own paranoia, based on past reports that he gave of his wife, I prayed over the food and then ate. Whatever happened, my prayer did not bring immediate victory. I left there hoping all was well.

I went to work the following morning. I felt I wanted to go do a bowel movement at about 9:30 a.m. In the process of relieving myself, I realized I was now experiencing rectal bleeding. The feeling was as if I had been cut with pieces of glass splinters.

Only God could divinely heal and deliver me from such danger. I later learned that that was a trick used by people to kill someone. I was in the restroom for nearly two hours. Upon returning to my office, I slumped down into my chair. My coworkers and supervisors got my attention, as they detected something was radically wrong with me.

It was totally out of character for me to be in the office so late and have my field partner waiting for me. I was employed by the Department of Housing Preservation and Development of the city in which I lived. I was field personnel. My previous day's work would have taken me no longer than one hour to complete, and then back to the field we would go.

Leaving the office the morning in question, I was delayed until 11:00 a.m. This attack, like others, was swept away by the power of the almighty God. Bowing my head on my desk, I prayed. My supervisor insisted that I go home and check in with a doctor. I refused and adamantly went and did my field work. I never experienced any severe pain.

These experiences have taught me valuable lessons. When one is born again into the family of God, one immediately becomes a soldier in training. There is no place for complacency. Paul, in admonishing his spiritual son, wrote, "Fight the good fight of faith, lay hold on eternal life, where unto thou art also called, and hast professed a good profession before many witnesses" (1 Timothy 6:12).

God has always been calling His children who are living on the earth to be on assignment for Him. The great thing about such assignment is that He has never assigned an unaccomplishable task. He sends you and me because He knows us. If we fail to take on our responsibilities, it will bother our spirit until we know that we are different from the people of the world.

To succeed in any other person's appointed assignment is almost impossible. Jehovah will show us what to do, even if by obscured vision. When we stay focused and with an upright heart, He will shine through us.

In my quest for the deliverance of these less-fortunate brethren, the Lord spoke to me. He took me, in the book of Revelation, to the past and then to the present. The Spirit of the Lord interrogated me. This interrogation led me back to the root of our ancestors' spiritual imprisonment.

The Spirit brought a holiday celebration to me, with all of its gory scenes. Then in questioning me, He asked, "Do you think that these scenes were meant to be for your entertainment? Do you remember what Jesus said about secrets that should be made known?"

I went and checked what He mentioned in Mark 4:22: "For there is nothing hid, which shall not be revealed or manifested; neither was anything kept secret, but that it should not come abroad."

I began to probe into the thoughts that flooded my mind. Then I understood that in order to keep a man, a family, a race, or a nation in financial bondage, blood has to be offered, on a continual basis. These are the demands that were set by the evil forces.

Those kinds of ancient practices prevailed because God's people have failed to live in His presence. They have refused to worship and praise Him uninhibitedly. In this generation, the younger people are not afraid, or ashamed, to get up on the stages with all of their academic achievements and shout the praises of God with all of their strength.

This generation will get the victory over Satan. They shall see the face of God. Hallelujah! The people who lived in Jeremiah's days were oppressed by their enemies around and about them. This caused him great concern. In his quest to bring or to maintain God consciousness among the nation of Israel, his messages from God were rejected.

They caught the prophet and threw him into a dungeon. In his expository deliveries, Jeremiah, who was God's spokesman, was rejected by his people. In his deliveries, he managed to ruffle the feathers of the authorities.

This got him into the slime pit, but God never left him there. God is faithful, and He will always come through to aid his suffering children. Our God is a good God. He is awe-inspiring. He is Jehovah. Almighty is He! His goodness never fails, and to those who love and fear Him, He will always be with them.

The teacher admonished us, "The fear of the Lord tendeth to life, and he that have it shall abide satisfied; he shall not be visited with evil" (Proverbs 19:23). God is omnipresent. "For the eyes of the Lord run to and fro throughout the whole earth, to show Himself strong on behalf of them whose heart is perfect toward Him" (2 Chronicles 16:9a).

King Asa forgot his past victories, which he could have only gotten because he trusted in the God of his fathers. When he went to acquire the help of the king of Syria without consulting God, he forfeited the protection that God had put in place for His children.

Sometimes our experiences do not always coincide with our expectations. They may even cause us to second-guess our former convictions. But if we keep on the trail, we shall end up at the promised destination. The children of Israel tempted God by questioning His ability to provide for them in time of famine.

They said, "Behold, he smote the rock, and the waters gushed out, and the Streams overflowed. Can He give bread also? Can He provide flesh for His people? Therefore, the Lord heard this, and was wroth; so a fire was kindled against Israel" (Psalm 78:20–21).

God has no pleasure in the disposition of His children's mistrust and lack of faith in Him. He told us to acknowledge Him in everything we do and that He would give us proper direction.

TWELVE
FILLING A VOID IN MY LIFE

THE NEED IN my life back in the 1980s was one of emptiness and a void. This great need allowed me to consult God. The enemy tried to fill it with his substitute, but by the Holy Spirit's discernment, I was able to make a quality decision. In this, I proved the faithfulness of God toward His promise in His words.

I fasted and prayed, seeking God for the right mate to complement my life. I knew He already had the answers to my prayers. This was one of the most outstanding times in my Christian life. I was living alone, but I was not lonely.

There were times when I was having my devotions, and I became aware of the presence of someone other than myself. I became too timid to open my eyes thinking I would see heavenly beings in my room. The presence of the Lord became so evident it erased my doubts and stimulated my confidence in Him.

The assurance that I received in my spirit that my prayers were answered could only be topped by God sending His messengers in physical form to confirm His response. I prayed earnestly for God to provide me with a mate. I requested a woman who loved and obeyed God more than her own fleshly desires.

I had already painted a picture of her in my mind and presented it to God in prayer. I was very specific and practical. I had her measurements, her academic abilities, and her profiling written down. I found out rather quickly that I could not ever challenge God on any account that He could not deliver.

He miraculously brought Grace into my life. Jehovah God will make us winners in life's games when we fully trust in Him. He wrote the game and the rules of the game. He knows the game too well to lose at it. The perfect picture of this woman did not take Him long to present to me.

Grace was the most unique woman that I had ever met in the church world—second only to my darling mother. She measured up to the minutest details, and for sure, she superseded my expectations. Like Job, I could not stand up to the divine challenges. So I said, "I will lay my hands upon my mouth."

Grace was very witty and wise. She was the personification of beauty itself. If one were asked to define beauty, then such a one could physically place Grace Brown-Dixon where the answer should be and would be correct. I asked the Lord to give me a woman whose measurements were thirty-four, twenty-eight, thirty-six. When I met Grace, she fit the measurements perfectly to a "T."

I reflected on my dad's wisdom that impressed me over the years. He was a very brilliant man. When I met Grace, I met one of the brilliant minds of our times. She was highly gifted and favored by God. I believe that when Grace made a request to man or to the Lord, God sent out all His reserved angels, and they got the job done.

Not only were they sent to get the job done, but time, for the most part, was erased from the equation. Whenever she encountered an important project, viewed by some to be impossible, the words "No" or "I cannot" had no part to play once she presented her request. Heaven stood at attention, the White House bowed to her requests, and the pheasants rose up to honor her.

"Who is this woman, or who are you?" were commonly asked questions. She was almost impenetrable to evil thoughts or darts from the enemy. When God gave her to me to be my wife, it was as if He said, "Simeon, here is my heart." She was ever so loving, enduring, and forgiving to all.

One description of her was "She had to be an angel wrapped in human flesh." Grace had no tolerance for evil speaking. She was a pattern of my dear mother. They both believed that if someone had done ninety-nine evil things to you, yet returned and intentionally or unintentionally did one good thing for you, all the evil things should be erased.

Oh, did my mother chorus those words in my brain! Grace had many battles in her short lifetime. Her coworkers coveted her, hated her, and hurt her immensely. Families and so-called friends alike hurt her most deeply. She cared deeply; therefore, she hurt deeply. That was a statement she repeated often.

Amid all of the disappointments, she kept on loving, caring, and cherishing, helping them heal from their own self-inflicted wounds. She was a keeper of the flame, a lifter of the torch, and a barer of her fellow man's burdens.

As soon as she detected the dimness of someone's flame in her relationships, she concocted a plan to rekindle the flames. If there were any degree of fear that could have affected her faith, it was cunningly fed to her by people whom she misjudged to be forthright in the faith. She had such faith and such tenacity that the impossibilities became possible.

THIRTEEN
CHOOSING A HOUSE

BUYING HER A house seemed impossible, given our employment status. We were in a lease purchase agreement. The end of the leasing period was fast approaching. I did not have a job, and my business was doing rather poorly. Despite all the negative aspects of our situation, we applied for a mortgage, which we were denied.

We tried another mortgage company twice, and they denied us also. We were gripped by the vice of desperation because we were about to be dispossessed from the house in which we resided. We prayed and believed God. Someone who knew my wife decided to give me a job to finish a basement. While I was working for my new client, she asked me, "Do you own your own home?"

"Not yet," I replied.

I told her of our plight. She encouraged me to look beyond all of those negative experiences and start afresh. She said to me, "Why don't you go right now and look around in this subdivision to see if you find a house that you like? Probably the builder will work with you."

I reluctantly went and looked around. I saw what I wanted as I looked at the first building I went into. It was in the process of building and was about 50 percent completed. I shared the new encounter with Grace after reaching home. This was a welcome idea to her.

Grace was one of those people who knew how to recognize a moment or a time that was impregnated with God's rich favors. She possessed the extra perception that enabled her to see possibilities conquering impossibilities.

She eagerly, said to me, "Take me over there." This I did, and she expressed her excitement and like for the area—eventually for what would become our home. Her minor struggle in perceiving what the completed product would look like was short-lived.

It did not take long for the obscurities to be erased and for her to place trust in my better-valued judgment in the field of building construction. We met with the builders. She had some ideas relating to her personal design, which she needed to establish.

Surprisingly, she instructed the builders on a different interior layout of the house. Some walls were eliminated, and fancy decorative wood columns were installed. The house came with a large den and kitchen. The den became our family altar.

Everyone who visited was introduced to the family gatherings. Hands were laid on them, or a circle was formed before prayers. Grace was born with natural decorating skills. She sketched her own patterns and purchased her own designer drapes as well.

Whenever we both traveled to the stores, we dispatched singularly, choosing the same item when we were back together. We were simultaneous in a lot of these shopping sprees, where we had similar experiences.

We never tried to make any family-associated decision without consulting with each other. We realized that if it pleased the Lord, then it pleased us. We did not have a lot of money, but God (Jehovah Jireh) met our every last need.

Grace loved the presence of God more than I can report. She was a person who prayed silently but intensely. She loved people like herself. She gave expecting nothing in return. She recognized my God-given ability to pray and faith in God so she was always volunteering me to pray for people or over situations that bothered her.

FOURTEEN
THE BATTLE WITH BREAST CANCER

SATAN HAS NO regard for God or His people. The fearlessness and blatant disregard of the devil for the ultimate authority and power of God is reported in the Holy Scriptures. Genesis 3:1–5 records,

> Now the serpent was more subtle than any other beast of the field which the Lord God hath made.
>
> And he said unto the woman, yea, hath God said, ye shall not eat of every tree of the garden? And the woman said unto the serpent, we may eat of the fruits of the garden: But of the fruit of the tree which is in the midst of the garden, God hath said, ye shall not eat of it, neither touch it, lest we die.
>
> And the serpent said unto the woman, ye shall not surely die: For God doth know that in the day ye eat thereof, then your eyes shall be opened and ye shall be as gods, knowing good and evil.

Satan distorted the truth of God's word and thus brought confusion, distraction, rebellion, and death to the human race. We read also in Isaiah an account of Satan's involvement and orchestration of a revolt against God in heaven.

> How are thou fallen from heaven, O Lucifer, son of the morning? How are thou cut down to the ground, which did weaken the nations! For thou has said in thine heart, I will ascend into heaven, I will exalt my throne above the stars of God: I will sit also upon the mount of the congregation, in the sides of the north: I will ascend above the heights of the clouds; I will be like the Most High. (Isaiah 14:12–14)

"Pride goeth before destruction and a haughty spirit before a fall" (Proverbs 16:18).

The devil's pride is always getting him into trouble, and he never learns. He poured his efforts into stopping the redemptive plans of God for lost humanity. To accomplish this, the devil took Jesus up on a pinnacle and showed Him all the kingdoms of the world in hopes that he would get Jesus off the track. He told Him, "All of this can be yours if you will abandon your mission and join with me" (Paraphrase, see Matthew 4).

Children of the living God are all targets of the devil. Every child of God who will exercise his or her faith in God and His word is a danger of the kingdom of darkness. If you are a target, you could be hit! You can die simply because it is said unto all living human beings, "It is appointed unto men once to die …"

Grace's battle began when she detected a small lump in her left breast. She asked me to check to see if I could discover what she had moments before detected. My findings were conclusive.

After a visit with her doctor, the conclusion was the same. The recommended regimens began. We made multiple trips to and from the doctor's offices, clinics, and hospital emergency rooms. We spent many nights in the hospital.

I witnessed the horror of the deadening grip of this dreaded monster. Shortly after the regimens of chemotherapy started, she lost all her hair. The doctors decided to do a mastectomy, but she persuaded them to perform a lumpectomy instead.

After surgery, the doctors gave her a clean report. There were no more cancer cells in her body. She was in remission for approximately one year. In the summer of 1997, she requested that I check a spot in the center of her left breast. I tried to be evasive, but she persisted.

"I do not like this," she said. "I think I need to make another appointment to see the doctor." So we concluded. Back to the doctor we went. All the oncologists confirmed that the cancer had returned. The devil had revamped. The battle returned, and we stood our ground.

The believers fasted collectively and individually. We refused to lie down and die. We were constantly reminded that God will give the victory. Grace had a relentless faith. The lesion grew so large so that from a distance those who did not know her thought she had three breasts.

It was agonizing to watch her go through episode after episode of unbearable pain, day in and day out. Every three days after the chemotherapy treatment, regurgitation set in. Most everything she swallowed came back up. This condition drained her of her energy and strength. I had to help her to and from the bathroom.

Taking care of her became my full-time job. The marital vow became a reality: "For better or worse." As in Job's case, God put me by her side, and I cared for her moment by moment.

Sometimes the short walk to the bathroom became challenging, like a mile's journey. She sometimes ran out of energy or endurance. I then got on the task of restoring sanity and comfort. As agonizing as the situation was, nothing could quench Grace's faith in God.

She was a public relations person. Freelancing from home, she kept up with the phone calls, letter writings, and sometimes consultations. She always insisted on getting things done in excellence. She did favors for her church and other entities.

The ministers and pastors of the church prayed for her constantly. In the middle of December 1997, we got a call from one of the pastors of the church, inquiring about her well-being. After she reported her condition to him, he told her that the Lord had spoken to him, telling him that it was time he came and prayed for Grace Brown-Dixon.

He invited us to come to his office. We went as invited. The pastor counseled with us in the word of God and then prayed. After prayer, he prophesied to us that the Lord said that in two weeks, "that thing would be gone."

We went home believing the prophet of the Lord. One week went by, and nothing happened. The second week came, and with great anticipation, we looked for a miracle. One evening, after I went home from work, she called me into the bathroom. With a big grin on her face, she opened her robe and said, "Don't be rude. Take a look."

I was totally amazed. I burst out in praise and thanksgiving to God. The lesion had shrunk to about two-thirds of its size. The shrinking continued gradually. By the end of December, it was totally gone.

In 1998, we had the happiest New Year we had ever had. She suddenly became a celebrity. She appeared on the television morning show, testified on other networks, and did interviews on the radio and in the newspapers. God gave us the unmistakable miracle. This confirms His words in Genesis 18:14: "Is anything too hard for the Lord?"

In February the following year, she went for her regular checkup. We sat in the doctor's office awaiting his arrival. As he walked in, he saw the smile on Grace's face. He eagerly inquired, "Is everything all right?"

"Yes, Doctor," she replied.

The doctor began his routine examination. "Will you remove your shirt for me, please?" he asked. And in slow motion, she removed her shirt. This Jewish doctor, who was the chief oncologist of the area, with clenched fists raised above his head, shouted, *"Merry Christmas!"* That mass was gone. The cancer was gone, and she was healed miraculously.

Having read so many real-life testimonies of the unmistakable, miracle-working power of God, we too have joined the myriads who have left their witness on the recorded history of the ages that our God "is able to do exceedingly, abundantly, above all that we ask or think" (Ephesians 3:20).